"Reggie Dabbs is a unique voice to this generation. The stories and principles you encounter in this book not only will inspire you but also will lead you on a journey to the core elements of life—and the potential therein to change."

—Mark Batterson
Best-selling author, *In a Pit with a Lion on a Snowy Day, Wild Goose Chase,* and *Primal;* and lead pastor, National Community Church, Washington, DC

"Reggie Dabbs's communication style spans generations. His engaging demeanor, biblical perspective, and phenomenal life story have given him an overcoming spirit that would challenge and encourage even the most downcast soul."

—Brian Houston
Senior pastor, Hillsong Church, Australia

"Reggie Dabbs is one of the strongest, most influential voices God has raised up to speak to this generation. He carries a special anointing to touch vulnerable hearts in desperate need of God's love. You will be deeply blessed as you read through each page of this book. His life story can be summarized in one word: *miraculous!*"

—Jentezen Franklin
Senior pastor, Free Chapel; and *New York Times* best-selling author, *Fasting*

"I love Reggie Dabbs because he is the same on stage and off; he is the real deal. You're going to love this book!"

—Michael Tait
Grammy Award–winning recording artist; lead vocalist, Newsboys; and former dc Talk member

"Reggie Dabbs is one of the most influential speakers of the 21st century. Reggie's life has inspired millions across the globe. He has a unique gift and anointing; this book will revolutionize your life! It is a must-read, and it will change your future."

—Russell Evans
Founder, Planetshakers,
Melbourne, Australia

"Why do untold numbers of people listen to Reggie Dabbs speak every year? Read this riveting book about the man and his mission. You will find your voice. You will learn your true identity. Most of all, you will discover your God-dreamed destiny. With God, all things are possible!"

—Dr. George O. Wood
General superintendent,
Assemblies of God

"Through his raw and real way of speaking, Reggie unabashedly shares the gospel and his life experiences to challenge and change our generation of young people for Christ. Every parent, youth leader, and teacher should read this book. It's an honor to call him my friend and to serve alongside his ministry through many conferences around the world."

—Israel Houghton
Grammy Award–winning artist
and international worship leader

"My friend Reggie Dabbs has had many times in his life when he could have given up and surrendered to difficult circumstances, but instead he has risen up and stepped into the calling that God has for his life. Through his fiery, passionate testimony, Reggie has impacted multitudes of lives worldwide while inspiring people to live a life of excellence. His story will encourage you that no matter your background, God has a plan and purpose for your life."

—John Bevere
Author and speaker, Messenger
International, Colorado Springs/
Australia/United Kingdom

"Through who he is and the message he speaks, Reggie has the unique ability to break down walls and barriers around the hardest of hearts. When you are around him, whether in a stadium of thousands or in a room with a few, you see someone with an immense passion for God and people. You can't help but be impacted by it."

—Sam Monk
Lead pastor, Equippers Church,
New Zealand and Europe

"Not only is Reggie Dabbs the *best* student communicator alive, his message is even greater: God can lift your life out of any circumstance and fill it with his destiny and purpose!"

—Tom Madden
International director,
Youth and Discipleship, Church of God

"Reggie Dabbs is not only an incredible minister of the gospel but also a dear friend who inspires me with his testimony and ability to reach a cross-cultural generation that is searching for the truth in life. Reggie's heart for the hurting and broken is a true measure of the message of the cross, and his ability to communicate with hilarity is captivating. Reggie is absolutely the real deal with a real message of hope!"

—Ricardo
Grammy-nominated, Dove Award–winning
worship leader and recording artist

"In the city and in the country, a school assembly in a gymnasium, a crusade in the biggest of stadiums, an indigenous outback community, or with the teenager in the shopping mall . . . Reggie's passion to bring hope to a generation is truly inspiring and transforming. His testimony, humour, and love for people leave an indelible mark wherever he goes. The impact of Christ on his life brings hope to all.

"I have heard Reggie say in hundreds of school assembly programs, 'You can't change your past, but you can change your future.' So true and, Reggie, you have changed our future . . . for the better!"

—Paul Geerling
Director, National Youth Alive, Australia

"The very first time I heard Reggie speak was in a huge room full of young people who would normally be anything *but* attentive when hearing a speaker. But you could have heard a pin drop as he shared his heart and the incredible story of his life thus far. The room swayed between silence and raucous laughter, and as I grew to know, this *is* Reggie's amazing gift. Through this book I *know* your heart will be moved with compassion and stirred to action. Be blessed in the reading as you get to know the heart, mission, and passion of my friend Reggie Dabbs."

—Darlene Zschech
Award-winning songwriter,
worship leader, pastor, speaker,
and founder, Hope Rwanda

"There really is only one Reggie Dabbs. He is unique . . . I would daresay, a phenomenon! His story is an inspiration. His energy is inexhaustible, and his legacy in our nation profound. He has been a reference point for a generation who says, 'If Reggie made it, so can I!' We love Reggie Dabbs and know that this book will be a source of great encouragement to all who read it."

—Wayne Alcorn
National president, Australian
Christian Churches; and senior pastor,
City Church, Brisbane, Australia

"I've known Reggie for ten years. Every time I see him—whether backstage at a convention center, by chance in an airport, or while he's on stage playing sax—I smile. He's that kind of guy—the kind you can't be around without feeling a bit of sunshine."

—David Crowder
Award-winning songwriter and
worship leader; and lead vocalist,
David Crowder Band

"Reggie offers convincing examples of faith in action and God's power to love and heal all wounds . . . presents a unique brand of hope."

—*Booklist*

REGGIE

To my BACK DOOR BABIES!

Love,

Jeff

REGGIE

YOU CAN'T CHANGE YOUR PAST, BUT YOU CAN CHANGE YOUR FUTURE

REGGIE DABBS
WITH JOHN DRIVER

THOMAS NELSON
Since 1798

NASHVILLE   DALLAS   MEXICO CITY   RIO DE JANEIRO

Published in Nashville, Tennessee, by Thomas Nelson, Inc. Thomas Nelson, Inc. is a registered trademark of Thomas Nelson, Inc.

Thomas Nelson, Inc. titles may be purchased in bulk for educational, business, fund-raising, or sales promotional use. For information, please e-mail SpecialMarkets@ ThomasNelson.com.

Unless otherwise noted, Scripture quotations are taken from the New King James Version®. © 1982 by Thomas Nelson, Inc. Used by permission. All rights reserved.

Scripture quotations marked NLT are from the Holy Bible, New Living Translation. © 1996. Used by permission of Tyndale House Publishers, Inc., Wheaton, Illinois 60189. All rights reserved.

Page design by Mark L. Mabry

Library of Congress Cataloging-in-Publication Data

Dabbs, Reggie.
  Reggie : you can't change your past, but you can change your future / Reggie Dabbs with John Driver.
    p. cm.
  Includes bibliographical references.
  ISBN 978-0-8499-4626-4 (pbk.)
  1. Dabbs, Reggie. 2. Christian biography. 3. Christian life. I. Driver, John, 1978– II. Title. III. Title: You can't change your past, but you can change your future.
  BR1725.D324A3 2010
  277.3'082092—dc22
  [B]

Printed in the United States of America

11 12 13 14 15 RRD 5 4 3

To my parents, William (Bill) and
Leila Dabbs. You didn't just adopt
me; you showed me how to live.

CONTENTS

ACKNOWLEDGMENTS

Thanks to all the people whose names are mentioned or unmentioned in this book and have been a part of my story. Thanks to all the educators, mentors, and friends who helped me at various times in my life: Dr. Robert Spence, Dr. Don Argue, Dr. Don Myer, and Dr. Gordon Anderson; Tom Greene, Larry Liebe, Sister Alice Jane Shaeffer-Blythe, Don and Janice Wilburn, Reverend Billy Mills, Jack Simon, Pastor Dan Betzer, Tom Madden, Gerald Ogg (you are greatly missed), and Dr. Charles and Lil McKinney. Special thanks to my extended family, the congregation of First Assembly of God in Ft. Myers, Florida. To Preston Centuolo, Richard Baker, Phil Brake, and Warren E. Shelton: we are the band of brothers who always has been, always will be, and even in heaven will still be together.

Thanks to Paul Geerling, Monty and Georgia Nidiffer, Kevin Norwood, Gary Sapp, Rich Wilkerson, Glen Berteau, Joe White, Erwin McManus, Bishop Joseph Garlington, The Katinas, and Judah Smith. Thanks also to Russell and Sam Evans at Planetshakers in Australia, Sam Monk and the Equipper Church family, Harold Velasquez, Harry Thomas at Creation Festival, Jentezen Franklin, the men and leaders of Promise Keepers, John Bevere, and the Assemblies of God.

To the incredible team at Thomas Nelson, thanks for believing in a man who didn't have an agent or a lawyer—who literally came to you out of the dark. May God put his hand on this book so that it will change lives around the world.

Andrew Wharton, from the backwoods of youth camp when

we were kids, to the halls of our college dorm, to now, you've always been a man whom I consider a great friend. Thanks for your vision to help make this book happen. Thank you, Life Assembly in Mt. Juliet, Tennessee. To my coauthor, John Driver: you literally became Reggie Dabbs . . . and only God can save you from this moment. I love you, brother.

Finally, to my wife, Michele. Thank you for standing by me and with me through the thick and thin of this crazy life we live. Your love has been my anchor and the best part of my story. To my son, Dominic, I could not be any prouder of the man you've become. Being your daddy is an adventure I will always cherish.

—Reggie Dabbs

To my incredible wife, Laura. I could never express my thankfulness for the countless times you not only tolerated but graciously celebrated our adventures in ministry, especially my unlikely call to write. The past decade—chocked full of late nights at my computer—is a direct reflection of the selflessness and strength you've infused into me. You are my best friend, and I fall more in love with you with each passing day. It's you and me against the world!

Sadie, you're Daddy's joy and always will be. I can't wait to see the woman you will become. Thanks to my family, the Drivers and the Canadas. To my friend and mentor, Andrew Wharton, I'm here only because you have poured energy, vulnerability, and opportunity into my life. Jonnie Wethington, you've been my best friend through years of constant change, and we've laughed the entire time. To my friend, Roy Stone, our hours of logos and laughter have been one of my favorite parts of ministry. Jeffrey Holland, you are truly a friend like no other—dinner is on me. Chris Long, thanks for walking this project to places we never could go on our own. To the rest of my family and friends (mentioned and unmentioned), "thanks" will never be enough.

Special thanks to my incredible sister, Julie; Giovanna Gomez; Pat Zimmerly; Jann Saulsberry; Terry and "Sam" Allen; Chuck and Laurie Lester; and the many others who have encouraged me in, read, and proofread my many writing endeavors over the years. Thank you, Life Assembly—you truly are the Greatest Church in America, and I love being one of your pastors. To the innumerable students (many who are now adults) who have listened to me ramble on all these years, you are more than just my proving ground; you are still my passion, and I thank God for the opportunity to be involved in your lives.

Thanks to the incredible staff and now friends of Thomas Nelson: you've been a joy to work with—thanks for believing in us. Mark Batterson, thanks for "calling it out" in me. Finally, thank you, Reggie, for partnering with me and giving me the opportunity to use my gift to craft another expression of your amazing story for the world. You're a great friend, and I got yo' back!

—John Driver

CHAPTER 1

THE PIGSKIN POET
KNOW YOUR STORY

A REALITY CHECK

> I don't have to know your name to know your pain . . .
>   I have my own.
> I don't have to see your home to know your shame . . .
>   I have my own.
> But someone loved me just the way I am,
> and someone loves you just the way you are.

I have recited this particular stanza to millions of people on every continent of the globe, even Antarctica! People so small they think no one sees them. People so much larger-than-life they sometimes forget the world is not, in fact, revolving around them. It does not matter who it is; these words mean something for everyone.

The author of this little piece of poetry may surprise you a bit. Yeah, that's right . . . it was me! Hi, I'm Reggie.

You should probably know that I am considered one of the most popular public school and motivational speakers in the world. These are not self-proclaimed titles. A self-proclaimed title might be "The Ultimate Ice-Cream-Eating Champion of the Universe," and I wear my cone-shaped crown with pride! Nevertheless, each year I speak to more than 2.5 million students face-to-face. Little faces. Dirty faces. Hopeless faces. Faces that wear invisible masks to hide their anguish. Faces that reflect stories of heartache and despair that are beyond comprehension. Faces of apathy.

I meet these faces every day. I speak to them in huge assemblies and sometimes in smaller, quieter venues. The size of the room does not matter; the size of the truth in this poem does. Why? In it is the key to helping wounded kids—and wounded people in general—understand that they are not alone in their pain. Someone cares. Someone loves them. Someone wants to be their *Daddy* when their real daddies have rejected, abused, and abandoned them. Over the past decade I have been called Daddy by more of these precious students than I could ever recall. In letters. In e-mails. In Facebook messages. In person. Even though I may not tuck them in at night or hand them lunch money before they get on the bus, you can rest assured that they have a father (in more ways than one) who loves them. You see, understanding my story helps them delve deeper into their own stories and rise above the tragedy of living in this nasty world.

You cannot change what has already happened. Good or bad, what is behind you is finished—you cannot take it back. That is a fact we all know, except maybe those who are spending their lives trying to get their DeLoreans up to eighty-eight miles per hour! The rest of us, though, live in reality. If we were to take an honest look within, we would all admit that the "reality house" does not always have the best view. Sometimes we pull back the drapes only to find a brick wall. *Bummer.* For most of us, our world is skewed by the reality of what dominates our vantage points. Our shortcomings. Our weaknesses. Our ineptitudes. Our fears. Our insecurities. Our inescapable family situations. Our pasts. So we usually just pull the drapes, turn on the television, grab a quart of Ben & Jerry's ice cream, and let ourselves get whisked away into someone else's reality.

Hmmm . . . I wonder why reality television is such a huge part of our culture? No doubt, we are mesmerized by the prospect of other people's realities being better places to live than our own. We long for their world, lusting for it with all we have within us. We fantasize about what it would be like to walk in their more expensive shoes, to drive their luxury cars, to sleep in their perfectly made beds. The grass is always greener, and whatnot. If I had their life, then my life would be livable. I would not have these scars. I would not have this home life. This marriage. This addiction. This disease. This crippling fear of movement. This past.

You can't change your past, but you *can* change your future by changing your present reality. The reality you have the potential to experience is not someone else's either; it is designed to fit you perfectly as if a master Italian tailor has taken your exact measurements and produced a personal masterpiece that is just your size. That is what I want for you. That is what I want for me.

In this book I have opened up my heart by honestly and candidly revealing some key details of my own life story. At times

> YOU CANNOT CHANGE WHAT HAS ALREADY HAPPENED. GOOD OR BAD, WHAT IS BEHIND YOU IS FINISHED—YOU CANNOT TAKE IT BACK.

I skip around, but the "big stuff" does come in some semblance of order. Simultaneously I share some anecdotes and ideas that will bring symmetry to my personal narrative. Some are humorous; others may make your eyes glisten a bit. But as we go along, my goal is to explore ten specific aspects of life that I believe are keys to finding the *present* process that can renovate our *futures*. The following pages will not magically produce the fulfillment of these truths in you, but they hopefully will jump-start some dead batteries that might be under your mental and emotional hoods.

I cannot change your reality, but I would love to journey with you through it. By the time you close this book, I hope you will have stumbled upon what it means to find a *new* reality by coming to grips with your story, your truth, your pain, your hero, your choices, your voice, your name, your passion, your future, and your Father. Let's begin the journey to knowing your own story by taking a look at mine.

PIGSKIN POET

In 1980 a young, handsome black boy of sixteen—that would be *me*—found himself living in Knoxville, Tennessee, home of the

Tennessee Volunteers. Knoxville was the ultimate southern football town. I attended Fulton High School on the north side; it is no surprise that I found some of my adolescent identity in football.

Why football? Uh, if you knew my size, you would understand. I was not exactly going to make it in ballet, although I can still fit into the tights I wore in high school. Seriously, football was just my speed. With my height and weight, I could pulverize anyone who dared to cross my path. Put pads on me, and I was in heaven!

If you have ever seen Adam Sandler in the movie *The Waterboy*, then you should understand why football was an escape for me. Just like Bobby Boucher, I found ways to visualize and attack. Who were the objects of my aggression? Every kid who had teased me about my weight over the years. Every locker room moron who had made a stupid joke about my family. Every skinny little punk who had ever smarted off to me became my opponent on that field—and I executed my wrath upon them play after play. Yeah, it was awesome!

Football was my ultimate passion, so you can imagine my dismay when my English teacher told us that we had to write a poem for an assignment. *Poetry? I eat poets!* But "Mrs. Grammarstein" made the unfortunate mistake of telling me to write about something I loved. Hence my first work of poetic art was skillfully penned. It went something like this:

[
I love football, yes I do.
I love football, how 'bout you?
]

I was shocked to learn that my teacher did not exactly share my enthusiasm. I guess my football poem was not quite

Shakespearean in its quality, so I was given a second chance—one of many second chances granted to me in this life. She instructed me to write a new poem that night and turn it in the next day.

When English class rolled around the following day, somehow, amidst the massive amount of responsibility and study in my life, I had forgotten to write the new poem. I have a little disorder called A . . . to the D . . . D D D . . . oh, sorry, I trailed off there for a second. You get the point.

So I grabbed a piece of paper and scribbled the first thing that came to my mind and turned it in. After a review of my seemingly ridiculous effort, she stood up and read the poem to the whole class—the same poem you read at the beginning of this chapter. She praised me for my obvious hard work and tedious planning. The secret was safe with me—now it is also safe with you.

That particular moment in my story was significant. Somewhere in the recesses of my adolescent mind—a mind cluttered with random and frequent thoughts of football, girls, and all-you-can-eat buffets—I saw a glimpse of my future. Why did that matter? Because in every school into which I walk all around this world, I encounter kids right smack-dab in the middle of their cluttered adolescence. Their generation is expected to do nothing but embrace a self-centered existence of trouble and insignificance. They are called ignorant, worthless, and other corrosive labels by influential figures in their lives. The words become self-fulfilling prophecies as these students live up (or should I say, live down) to the expectations.

NOT-SO-GREAT EXPECTATIONS

When kids realize they are not expected to be anything or do anything significant, their lives can become stagnant pools of distracted water. There is no flow—nothing of value coming in and nothing of value going out. We have taught a generation that their teen years are just "practice life." Sure, we might give it other names like "sowing wild oats" or "finding yourself," but what we are actually telling them is that what they are doing right now does not count.

That is where Reggie (that's me in third person) differs from the rest of the world. I tell students that the life they are living right now, at any age, is not at all a practice run—it counts. I am not saying that mistakes cannot be forgiven or that detours cannot be rerouted. I am saying that students in their teen years can positively influence the world *right now*! Conversely, they can also set themselves back for years to come, or even permanently, by their actions or inaction.

Just ask a young single mom or a sixteen-year-old drug addict. They will tell you their choices are already impacting their lives for the long haul. Or even more tragically, stand over the grave of a young man who checked out of this life early because at that exact moment he did not understand the value of who he was. Someone needs to tell these kids the truth, in many cases, before it is too late.

Sometimes when I am speaking, I randomly pick out four young men from the crowd—guys of random age, size, and ethnicity—and have them stand up. I then tell them that they are now all my sons, which is usually pretty humorous, especially if they are white. I have always wanted white kids! At this point you can bet their friends will begin to tease them and laugh. *Typical.* I tell them to ignore everyone around them for the next three minutes and just listen to the words I am about to speak into their lives. For these few moments only my sons and I are in the room.

I point to the first young man. "I've always loved nicknames; maybe that's why I want all of my children to have them. You, my son, will be called Champion." The room gets quieter as the kids assembled try to figure me out. I continue, "I want every person in this room who has lost a loved one to cancer to stand up."

Immediately there is an alarmingly loud reverberation of hundreds and hundreds of chairs squeaking or bleacher seats creaking as a great number of students slowly rise to their feet. A sobering shiver ripples through the now silent crowd. The impact of this modern plague hits home with kids who were laughing hysterically only thirty seconds earlier. I continue to speak to my Champion. "Somewhere in the recesses of *your* mind, there is buried the knowledge that will cure this epidemic. You don't realize it now, and maybe you think that you don't have what it takes, but listen to me, my son: I believe in you! You can do it!"

With no hesitation I turn to the next young man standing. "And you, I'll call you World Changer. Listen, son, sometimes I travel to the continent of Africa. There is one area of Africa so decimated by violence and bloodshed that I'm not allowed to be inside the borders after sunset. I literally have bodyguards who escort me the entire time. I begin speaking to kids in the twelfth grade at 6:30 a.m., and by the end of the day, I'm speaking to preschoolers."

The student is obviously curious about why I am telling him

such a long story while he is still just standing there. I don't miss a beat. "On a trip I took a few years ago, I had spoken all day long, and it was starting to get dark when a little boy took my hand, and through a combination of broken English and a translator, he asked me to come help him with his mother. His eyes were piercing, and my heart was moved. So with bodyguards in tow, I began walking across this field of wheat with this little boy toward his home, not knowing what I would find when we got there.

"Just ahead of us we saw that the wheat was flattened, so my bodyguards went ahead to check it out. They returned to inform me that the boy's mother had already died in the field.

"I turned around to walk away when I felt a little hand take hold of mine. In his best English my little friend whimpered, 'Will you help me bury my mother?'"

Pin drop. No one's talking now. The young man before me has suddenly forgotten the thousands of eyes on him. He is listening. "Son, somewhere inside you is the answer to the global decimation that is AIDS. You will end the issue. Your hands will heal the nations."

Next boy. "Your name is History Maker. From the deserts of Africa to the streets of New York City, there are millions of people starving to death. They lack clean water and adequate nutrition. But you, my son, you possess in your mind the ability to transform the science of agriculture. You will grow tomatoes as big as watermelons, and you will make miles of crops grow in the middle of deserts. You will solve the issue of world hunger."

Finally I turn to the last young man standing. "And last but certainly not least, your name is simply Legend. Your voice will transform people's lives. They will travel from hundreds and even thousands of miles around to hear the words from your lips. They will enter the room ready to give up—even to end their lives—but they will leave that same room with hope. Your words will mend the gaping wounds in the lives of a generation."

This is one of the solemn moments of my presentation for students—one of the few. It is solemn because most of those kids have never been exposed to the idea that they possess the potential to change the world. They think they are screwups. Misfits. Haphazard accidents stumbling through messy and mediocre lives.

Their age is irrelevant. Humanity itself is the common thread. They are you. They are your kids. They are me. They are my kids—kids that I want, even if no one else does.

THE TREASURE HUNTER

I did not start where I am today. I did not always possess the passion for students that now keeps me up at night. I started at the same place as most of the kids I just described: ground zero. Well, in my case, you might say I started at "ground negative."

That is the thing about life: you begin somewhere. Learning and accepting where you come from and what details of your story have initiated the sequence of events that has forged your path—the path that has led you to where you stand today—are the beginnings of the potential you have to make real changes to your present reality. Again, you cannot *change* the past, but you can *face it*. And you need to! It is impossible to live in *today* when your heart and mind still feel either painfully limited or foolishly overconfident by what happened *yesterday*. Either way, your story waits for you to acknowledge it. Within it is truth that needs to be brought inside from the cold of your past. That truth needs to live where you live—on the inside.

Don't panic; I'll go with you. For a minute, let's travel again back to my high school story and to the poem I scribbled on a scrap of paper in a moment of panic. When I recall that fateful day at Fulton High School when those words dripped improbably from my ballpoint pen, I am convinced there is hope for the kids I see every day. That moment in my story was a glimpse of a treasure few people in my life would have believed even existed. But it was there; and it *is* there in the lives of people all over this spinning globe. So what *is* this treasure they all possess?

It is hope. Hidden. Dormant. Buried in the recesses of their situations. But just like grass growing up through the cracks in a concrete sidewalk, hope can somehow break through toward the light. Unexpected. Against all odds. Sometimes the hardest of hearts will produce the greatest of champions. That is where I come in. I am like a concrete-crack gardener. I pour the water of love into the cracks of hopelessness. I see the poetry in the lives of the despondent. Sometimes their pants are sagging past their knees. Sometimes they come into the auditorium through metal detectors. Sometimes they wear school uniforms and get dropped off by moms driving BMWs. Sometimes their faces are pierced and every square inch of their bodies is tatted up. Sometimes they are guys; sometimes they are girls. Sometimes they speak with British or Australian accents. Sometimes they speak languages that I cannot understand (thank goodness for interpreters).

Why me? That's easy. I *was* them. Maybe I was *you*!

We all look different, but each of the present generations is screaming out in one collective cry for someone to bring them hope . . . to bring them love. Parents, peers, spouses, or even the most trusted of friends may not provide this kind of hope. The media and entertainment industries most certainly won't. There are those who are definitely trying to help, but the only person I can speak for is myself. The only person you can speak for is yourself. I want to illuminate this hope just as it was illuminated for me.

> EACH OF THE PRESENT GENERATIONS IS SCREAMING OUT IN ONE COLLECTIVE CRY FOR SOMEONE TO BRING THEM HOPE . . . TO BRING THEM LOVE.

My little poem taught me that light *can* break through . . . even when no one expects it to. It foreshadowed what I would do with my life, and it showed me there truly is treasure buried in the hearts of this generation . . . of every generation. And that includes you.

I've been hunting for it for quite some time now.

PAINFUL REVELATIONS

Much of my life is consumed with travel. Airports. Rental cars. Fast-food restaurants. I spend countless hours traipsing through cities by the light of GPS turn-by-turn directions. One of my favorite places to visit is England. I love the accent, although I am not much for reproducing it. I think the aura of a black man of my physique crashing into their culture has endeared me to the British.

In London I speak to so many thousands of students, they

have to rent an arena to hold them all. At the end of my presentation, there is sometimes an added segment for the kids called "Ask the American." It is basically an open-mic opportunity for the students to throw any and every fathomable question at me. I have gotten every kind of question from "What's the secret of life?" to "What's your favorite food?" My absolute favorite question was, "If you were a pigeon and you were going to take a poo, what would you poo on?" I told that inquisitive student that I would find the most expensive car in all of London and drop the mother lode on it! Ah, the gentle nuances of adolescent humor.

During one of these sessions a student asked me about my greatest regret. That was an easy one: second grade, on the way home from a parent-teacher conference. When you finish this book, you might disagree that this particular incident should be my greatest regret. Please understand that I only regret it because of the resulting pain that second-grade boy faced when he got his answer. And here is my story.

Second grade was not exactly my finest hour, unless you measure success by how many tubes of superglue can be used for the forces of evil. Superglue was my friend, though. Once, I superglued my best friend to his chair. When he stood up, his clothes didn't. It was one of the greatest moments of my life.

But the day of reckoning finally came. The teacher released us to the playground for a full day of play, which would usually send us skyrocketing into utter elation. However, the reason we were getting to play all day was that our teacher was going to be meeting with our parents. *Busted!*

From the monkey bars I saw my parents get out of their car and begin walking toward the school building; they were the first ones on the list. *Gulp.* Upon seeing my dad, one of the other kids pointed a freshly snotted finger in his direction and screamed, "King Kong!"

Yeah, that should let you know what my father looked like. Six feet, six inches, two hundred and sixty-five pounds of pure, intimidating *man*ness! I loved my dad, but I most definitely feared him as well. His voice resonated like thunder, and his belt struck like lightning. It is no wonder that, to this day, I have never tasted alcohol, cigarettes, or drugs. His threats of what would happen to me if I ever touched the stuff are still ringing in my mind. *Boy, if the drugs don't kill you, I will!*

When I said, "Yes, sir," you better believe I meant it!

At his side was the stunning antithesis of his girth. My mother was the most beautiful woman on the planet! That is not just the opinion of a nostalgic son. Everyone who saw her thought the same thing. Momma had a way of letting the beauty of physical appearance spill over into the other areas of her life. She was pretty in every way possible. Her beauty was my inspiration.

She had one word in particular that melted me. And there was a gentle sweetness to her tone that said as much as her actual words. When Momma said, "Baby," my cloudiest day found sunbeams, and my darkest night found light. She truly was the personification of sunshine.

The meeting with my parents and my teacher that day was a less-than-joyous event. I had to answer for my adhesive crimes and face the music. But something else that day suddenly became very apparent. I had not noticed it before that day, but my parents seemed to be significantly older than the other kids' parents. Since subtlety was an art that I had not really learned yet (and still haven't, for that matter), on the way home I simply piped up from the backseat, "Hey! Why are y'all old?"

That question was my greatest regret. It triggered a series of events that would forever change the course of my life. The ride home was uneventful, but after a few minutes at the house, I was called into the dining room. Any kid out there knows that it is never good to be called to the table when there is no food involved. Hey, if you don't smell something cooking, just run! It was a crucial piece of knowledge I had yet to learn.

I positioned myself at the table between my parents. "Son," my father said solemnly, "God has a plan for your life, and we're going to help you find it."

Even when the content of a conversation is over the head of a youngster, there is still no denying the power of the feeling in the room—that tangible tension detectable at any age. I did not understand at all what he was talking about, yet I was beginning to grasp the fact that I was in for more than I had bargained for. My dad continued, "Your mother has something that she needs to tell you."

Then it happened. My mother. My pillar of sweetness. My maternal champion. She began to weep bitterly. As a second grader I was terrified. Momma was the one who took care of *me* when *I* cried. She always told me that it was going to be okay. My world began spinning because if Momma was not okay, then something was terribly wrong!

One minute passed. Then two. Time stood still as my mother fought and failed to regain her composure. More time elapsed. The moment is so permanently sketched upon the canvas of my mind that I can remember the clock in the kitchen that day. It was a clock built into a little barn. I watched as the big hand moved ten times.

By that point, my father had repositioned himself next to his bride and was consoling her. My hands were sweating profusely, but my eyes refused to drip. There was a numbness setting in that left me strangely stoic. It was probably my childish brain's defense mechanism—a breaker that was automatically thrown when the circumstance at hand threatened to overload my emotional system.

Momma just could not seem to get there. Dad kept trying to comfort her. He continued encouraging her to tell me. Finally she pulled it together long enough to speak. She said two things that day that changed the course not only of my life but also of the millions of lives whom I have humbly had the opportunity to influence. The first was, "Reggie, you can't change your past; but you can change your future." There was the encouraging mom I knew. I felt relieved, not because any issues were resolved but simply because Momma was finally sounding like my mom.

Then the dagger came. "Reggie, the reason your father and I look so old is . . . Baby . . ."

I always loved it when my mom called me Baby.

My story was changing, but the direction of my life would never be able to change until I became acquainted with my story. It was a necessary scalpel that sliced through the first thin delicate layer of my identity. There were many more layers to come that would feel the blade.

"I'm not your real mother."

Questions for Individual and Group Reflection

1. What are your impressions of Reggie's high school poem?

   _____

   _____

2. Have you ever longed for someone else's reality? Why do you think we often do this?

   _____

   _____

3. Do you really think that other people's realities are the same to those people as are our impressions of their realities? Why or why not?

   _____

   _____

4. We can't change our pasts, but how can we change our futures?

   _____

   _____

5. How do the details of our own personal stories affect our viewpoints on the world and our lives?

   _____

   _____

6. How do people live up or live down to the expectations their peers, their families, or their cultures have for them? Explain.

_____

_____

7. What are your impressions of Reggie's speeches to the young men in his public school assemblies? How would the world change if people believed their stories could end up like the expectations Reggie gives to students?

_____

_____

8. Do you really believe light can break through and bring growth through the concrete cracks? What keeps us from believing in this kind of hope in others and in ourselves?

_____

_____

9. What details of your personal story define you? What events have shaped your personality and view of the world?

_____

_____

10. What can happen when we ignore the pertinent, even painful, details of our stories? What can happen when we acknowledge and learn from those details?

_____

_____

CHAPTER 2

TUESDAYS WITH REGGIE
KNOW YOUR TRUTH

ROLLER-COASTER REGGIE

We are all different. Yep, that is probably the understatement of the century! Some people are big. Some are small. Some are white. Some are black. Some are Asian. Some are Hispanic. But I don't see people in terms of race or color; I see them as food groups. Big surprise, I know.

Everybody I meet is just a different shade of chocolate. Walking through this life, I come across white chocolate, dark chocolate, and milk chocolate. It doesn't matter because at the end of the day, all chocolate is *good*! So every day I tell the various *chocolates* of the world how good they are and that they have value. That's what I do.

When I take the microphone in a public school assembly, I always tell the students that I have been brought in to talk to them about life—two life issues in particular. The first is that boys and girls are different. Somewhere in the back, I usually hear some sharp-tongued freshman pipe in with, "Nuh-uh! Mama said we were the same!"

Mama is wrong! The differences between the sexes are vast, but they begin with each person's morning routine. Boys and girls both stand over the sink to brush their teeth . . . well, hopefully. Inevitably, from time to time, that huge hunk of toothpaste that so desperately clings to those toothbrush bristles will take a dive into the sink. For the delicate females the answer to this problem is simple: squeeze the tube again and begin the process anew.

Guys? Eh, not so much. There will be no waste of precious, minty fluoride here. Men? We just scoop it up. That's right, scoop it up! Who cares if Dad shaved earlier that morning? So what if you go to your first-block class with whiskers on your teeth? Such is the way of the male psyche. I never said it was not a scary way.

The differences between the genders continue with this declaration: "Girls are better drivers than boys." You can only imagine the uproar of macho disdain that erupts from that statement. Here's how I prove it: Girls will run their cars off the road to avoid a deer. Bambi must be saved! Guys, we will run our cars off the road trying to hit that antlered sucker!

> GUYS SHOULD TREAT WOMEN WITH RESPECT BECAUSE THAT IS THE GREATEST THING A GUY CAN GIVE A GIRL.

Therefore, guys should treat women with respect because that is the greatest thing a guy can give a girl. He should open the door for her. He should pull out the chair for her—just not right before she sits down. When he comes to pick her up for a date, he should bring flowers. If he cannot afford flowers, he should just swing by the local cemetery on the way. (Hey, the people there will never know they are missing.) He should call her "honey," not "heifer"—she is a sweet woman, not a cow! *R-e-s-p-e-c-t.*

The second thing I tell the students is this: life is a roller coaster.

For me life is all about friends. Friends are wonderful. I have a lot of them—check out my Facebook page. But here is the thing about friends: they will talk you into things you would never do on your own.

Several years ago I found myself speaking at a conference in a major theme park. That is when the peer pressure began. My friends began heckling me to get on a roller coaster with them. I refused. They persisted. I relented.

Strapped into the fast death train of fun, I heard all too soon the universally familiar clicking of the car's upward climb, and I found my heart in my throat. Rounding the top of the first hill, the fun began. Up and down we flew, and I screamed like a girl— a very large black girl with a goatee. Then came the unthinkable: as we entered a vertical turn, the ride broke down, suspending us upside down in midair for several minutes. I would love to tell you that seeing all this was frightening, but I could not see a thing. Why? Well, my fat had flown up over my head, and my belly button was leaving a nice hickey on my forehead. But that was not the worst of it. The lady sitting behind me started throwing up—and the wind was blowing in my direction! That was a bad day.

> UP AND DOWN WE FLEW, AND I SCREAMED LIKE A GIRL—A VERY LARGE BLACK GIRL WITH A GOATEE.

Such is life, I suppose. Up and down we go. We have fun. We experience nausea. Sometimes it feels as though the ride is broken and we are just hanging there with no hope—no hope for marriages, no hope for graduation, no hope for living. Let me tell you what I tell students and adults alike week after week: When life hangs you upside down, you can rest assured that someone will fix the ride of life. The question is, will you still be on the ride when it restarts?

Remember the "Ask the American" program I participated in while in England? Once a young lady approached the microphone and apologized for the seriousness of her question. With a hushed crowd listening the girl asked me, "Reggie, do you ever wish that you weren't alive?"

My heart overflowed as I gave her my honest answer. "Yes, I do."

The day I learned the first few disturbing details of my life's story was the day I began to learn the truth. The funny thing about that truth was that it had always existed; I was just catching up with it. We are inclined to only think about the things to which we are exposed. Just like the European explorers who discovered a *new world* in the Americas, we are on a quest for truth. Interestingly enough, the continent they discovered was not new at all. It had been there all along. It really was just their knowledge of it that was new.

That is how truth works. We are not on a quest to create new truth. We are on a quest to discover *the* truth. The new world has always been there, yet it has remained hidden from our sight. However, just as those early explorers soon found out, the adventure of finding *new* truth brings with it a whole new world of challenges. Disease, inclement weather, hostile indigenous peoples, wild animals, and a host of other unknowns provided troubles that our forefathers had never dreamt.

But you know what? The truth that the Americas existed was worth it, even when colonists later began to settle here and found the process of survival harsh and grueling. That is the nature of truth: we need to know it even if it hurts. We need to know our truth.

MY PERSONAL TUESDAY

"I'm not your real mother." My heart sank when my mom uttered those fateful words to me. To a second grader, what could be more devastating than to hear that the woman you have always looked to as Momma is, in fact, not your real mother? I was crushed, and so was my mother . . . well, now my foster mother.

This piece of knowledge, along with much more to come, became the defining feature of my life. It caused me to question. To doubt. To face the realities of a harsh world. To feel rejection from the one who was supposed to love me the most. What hope was there for a boy whose own mother did not even want him?

It is what I call my *personal Tuesday*.

"Tuesday?" you might ask. "What's so bad about Tuesday?"

I'll explain. Before I do, though, let me make a disclaimer. The story I am about to reference may be recognizable to you. In fact, depending on your personal philosophy, belief, and experience, it might even be an eye-rolling affair for me to tell it. For now, do me a favor: suspend what thoughts may be floating around in that head of yours, and just let the ideas in the story stand for themselves, independent of your past experiences or preconceived notions. Just for a moment pretend you never before have heard the story. And even if you do not believe it, try to hear the point of what I am trying to convey.

A book I have been reading recounts the day the earth was fashioned (technically it took a week). What was the first accomplishment? How about the innovation of something simple, such as light itself? The Creator made light and caused it to be separated from the darkness. He called the light "day" and the darkness "night." At the end of this simple yet amazing feat, he made a profound observation about the light. He saw that "it was good."

Yeah, I would say it was good all right. Can you imagine life without light? "Good" is an incredible understatement. However, there was much more to come in the project of creation. The second day, he added to his own resourceful wonder with more inventive acts, but here's the kicker: he never indicated that they were good. Hmmm, interesting.

The third day came around. He separated the water and the land, and caused plants and trees to spring up all over the earth. If you are a fan of apples and oranges, then this is your day. Food sounds good to me! Apparently he, too, saw that it was good.

And so it went the following days of the week . . . six days of work with a one-day vacation to finish it all on the seventh day. Maybe he hit a few golf balls around the new greens he had just created—lucky Creator.

But, dude! What is the deal with day two? Was it a bad day? Were the things created on the second day worse than the other days? Of course not. They were all good! Just for argument's sake, though, maybe we can accept the fact that there are certain times in our lives when it is downright difficult to see any of the good that surrounds us. Sometimes it is just *Tuesday*, and things do not seem to be that *good*.

Maybe you can relate; I sure can. Maybe you feel as if you have been living in your own personal Tuesday for years now. Maybe things will not straighten out for you, and the ride of life seems as if it will never be fixed. Maybe you are like Bill Murray in *Groundhog Day*—for you, every day is a personal Tuesday.

Tuesday is the reason I spend much of my life traveling and speaking to students and adults all over this dark-watered globe—people trapped in their own Tuesdays.

WAITING BY THE DOOR

My son, Dominic, is my favorite person in the whole world. My boy! I would die for him. Bleed for him. Eat for him . . . and with him! He is a beast of a young man. A football specimen. I don't know *where* he gets it.

Dominic is in high school, and when he comes home, he has a definite ritual. First he hugs and kisses his mom. *Nice, son.* Next he pets his dog, Max. Then he runs to the refrigerator, throws his arms around it, and says, "I love you." Finally he looks at me and simply says, "'Sup, Dad?" Yeah, I love my boy.

But one day last year when he came home, something just seemed off. He kissed his mother, petted his dog, but completely skipped the refrigerator. I was nervous. He looked at me with weary eyes and said, "Dad, I'm kind of tired. I'm going to go ahead and go to bed." It was five thirty in the afternoon.

"You okay, son?" I asked. "Anything you want to talk about?"

"No, Dad. I'm fine." He mustered up a fake, conciliatory smile and moped off to his room.

Once his door was shut, I grabbed a book I had been reading, the dog, and a box of Ritz crackers. I kissed my wife and said, "Good night. I'll see you in the morning." It was only six o'clock. I plopped myself down on the floor in front of Dominic's door with my book and Max. There we waited.

I waited all night. Why did I sit there on that uncomfortable floor? I will tell you why: just in case he called my name. He never did. In fact he actually tripped over me the next morning on his way to the bathroom. The bottom line was my boy needed someone to be listening just in case he called out for help. How cool would that be! He rolls over and quietly whispers, "Dad?" Instantly I bust through the door like some comic-book Super Dad. "Yes, son?"

Okay, sure, it did not happen that way, but I hope I made my point. I was guessing that Dominic had been faced with a Tuesday-kind-of truth that day. It was hard to handle. It was not good, but it was a reality of his story.

We all need someone who waits with us through our Tuesdays, listens for our voices, and lingers at the doors of our issues. You need it. I need it. Sometimes, Tuesdays do not get any better; they simply must be endured. However, we were never intended to endure them alone—to walk in solitary darkness with no help from others.

I cannot wait outside the doors of the millions of students I speak to each year; I cannot even wait outside *your* door. But the truth remains: we all need someone to be listening for our cry. Why? Because if we get off the ride of life during our Tuesdays, we will miss what is coming the next day: something good!

A SAD TUESDAY STORY

I had a best friend when I was young whose real name I will not use here. Let's just call him Ryan. We did everything together. Got in trouble together. Played sports together. We were even top-secret spies, as evidenced by our really cool walkie-talkies.

Our friendship was awesome. But truth be told, Ryan's life was lived in a horrid Tuesday. His dad, you see, was an abusive drunk who beat up both Ryan and his mom on a regular basis. Ryan's only saving grace was *my* dad, who would get there as fast as he could to stop Ryan's family from getting hurt. That is where our walkie-talkies came in. Dad gave them to us so Ryan could let me know when things were getting bad at the house.

Of course, we also had lots of fun playing with them. He was G.I. Joe One, and I was G.I. Joe Two. I will never forget the night one of his calls came in.

"G.I. Joe Two! This is G.I. Joe One, come in! Come in!"

"G.I. Joe Two here!" I answered. "Do you need assistance?"

A long pause on the other end. "Too late."

His drunken father grabbed the walkie-talkie and said, "You want to know what I'm going to do to your friend?" Then he began to viciously beat my best friend with the antenna of our favorite toy until my father could get there to stop him.

Yeah, Ryan definitely lived in a perpetual Tuesday. We grew up, though (well, as much as can be expected). We were still great friends when we got to high school, but our paths began to diverge. As a freshman Ryan fell in with a group of seniors who found great amusement in getting him plastered . . . then laughing at him as he did stupid stuff in his drunken stupor. He was so desperate for the approval his dad never gave him that he just could not see that his "friends" were not really friends at all. I cannot count the number of nights I took him home when he had passed out.

One night Ryan called and asked me to come get him. When I arrived at the house where the party was going on, he was nowhere to be found. I heard water running in the bathroom. When I opened the door, my best friend was passed out in a pool of his own vomit. He was not breathing.

I performed CPR on him until the paramedics arrived, but he was gone. He had literally drowned in his own vomit, and I could not save him. From that day forward I have had to live with the fact that my best friend never made it out of his own personal Tuesday. He never saw the good of his Wednesday. He never found or faced the truth of his life; instead, he ran from it. Though I did not quite have the perspective then that I do now, I am determined to help people realize they do not have to die in the Tuesday of their predicaments, weaknesses, or setbacks. They can live. I can live.

You can live!

A PILL TOO HARD TO SWALLOW

I have told you the speech I give to my "sons," but I also give a speech to my "daughters." Instead of picking a few girls, as I do the guys, I usually select a whole row of them and have them stand together. Then I issue a blanket invitation that any of the girls in the room who want to be my daughter can stand as well. The number of girls looking for a daddy is staggering. The Daddy Speech begins, but this one is a bit more boisterous than the one I give to the boys. Those of you with daughters will understand.

> You are my daughters. You need to know one thing above all else: your daddy loves you! I will fight for you! I will hurt people for you, especially those punk little boys who come knocking at my door hoping for the privilege to take you on a

date. When they come to the door to meet me, I'll meet 'em, all right . . . as I clean my shotgun! And if they take you to the movies, you can look over your shoulder and see Daddy. And if that little punk wants to buy you popcorn, you can forget it! I'm the daddy, and I'll be buying the popcorn!

They all laugh, but then they get eerily quiet at the next part. "No matter where you go, Daddy will find you! If you're lost, Daddy won't rest until you are safe. If you make your bed in hell, Daddy will break down the door and rescue you. No matter what happens, your daddy will always love you! Always."

By now you can usually see tears streaming down a few pretty faces—faces longing for a daddy to tell them what I have told them. Faces stuck in the Tuesday of abuse and neglect. Faces looking anywhere for love and acceptance when they should have already found it at home. Faces etched with their own harsh truths, yet still desperate for new truth.

It reminds me of a true story of another young lady whom I never actually met or spoke to but who lived through her share of personal Tuesdays. Her name was Ruth. She married a man who died tragically just a few years into their marriage. Her mother-in-law was named Naomi. Naomi had another daughter-in-law whose husband died too. And if that were not enough, Naomi's own husband died as well. Now, that is a bad set of events. Three husbands. Three daddies. All gone. That's a very bad day!

Naomi was more than upset; she was devastated. Her words to her daughter-in-law Ruth proved the depth of her despair when she said, in effect, "This is a bitter pill for me to swallow— more bitter for me than for you . . . a hard blow." She went on to say something that just may be true for many people in our world, maybe even for you. She said, "May you be treated as kindly as you have dealt with the dead and with me."

Notice what Naomi said here: "the dead and me." She listed herself among said dead. In her mind life was already over. She was still breathing, but she was not living. She had resolved herself to a life of death. Maybe that is where you are; maybe that is the only reality you can see. I witness it every day in schools all over the world—those who have been dealt a severe blow and now feel as though the dirt of death is slowly piling up on the coffin of their existence. Buried alive in a situation that is unbearable.

But it does not have to be that way. Anyone who has heard this story knows that Naomi's life eventually saw much better days because someone loved her and came to her aid. Someone loves you too! Someone is speaking a message of love to the sons and daughters of the world. There is a Daddy who loves the babies. There is a Father who longs to hold them and protect them. There is healing for those who have faced the tragedies of life and love lost. There is hope—a truth chipping away at the walls of your hell to rescue you from the flames of rejection, hate, and abuse.

Tuesday will pass, but will you still be on the ride? I am pleading with a generation to hear a Daddy's plea to hold on and wait. Whatever the truth of your life may be, do not use the rope given to you to make a noose. Use it to climb up and out of where you are. Don't veg out, don't cop out, don't sit this one out! Don't hypnotize yourself with the television in the hope that reality will just fade away. Face your truth so you can find the next step that leads you through your own personal Tuesday. Hold on and keep climbing. Take it from one who understands the terrible truths of Tuesdays; you must *not* let go.

BACK AT THE KITCHEN TABLE

My personal Tuesday was just beginning. Mom's revelation to me that my parents were not actually my parents hit me like a sack of rocks. I began a journey of revelation that was far from what I had expected in my life. Over the following months and years, I began to learn the real story of the woman who did not want me as her son.

Her name was Vera, and she attended school on the north side of town in Knoxville. At the ripe old age of fourteen, she became pregnant with a little boy named Keith. He is my brother although I have never met him, and I have no idea where he is or what his life is like. The young mother gave birth to Keith and kept him while still living with her parents.

Her story became more complicated when she became pregnant again the next year . . . with twins. She went home and told her parents the news. They were furious with her as the sun set on that, no doubt, impossible day. The next morning she got up and went to school as usual, leaving her infant son in her parents' care. When the school bell rang, Vera made her way back home carrying a bag full of books and a heart full of worry. Little did she know, her Tuesday was just beginning.

She climbed the front porch steps only to hear the screaming of her little boy inside. As she opened the door, she beheld the unthinkable: the house was completely empty, except for her little baby, crying desperately for his mother.

They had moved while she was at school. They took everything. Furniture. Food. Appliances. They even took Vera's clothes with them. They left no note. No forwarding address. No hope. From that day forward she never saw or heard from her parents again.

Life had changed, and Vera was in way over her head. Pregnant. Unemployed. Single mother. Homeless. She dropped out of school and found her way to a halfway house, where she stayed until the twins were three months old. That was when the program director told her that the rules of the home prohibited them from staying because the children were too old.

Vera's options were simple. Simple but not easy. She could either give up her children to the Department of Children's Services and continue living at the home, or she could launch out on her own with her kids. She loved her kids. She decided to try it alone.

Someone helped her secure lodging at an old abandoned farm on the outskirts of town. She took her precious babies and moved them into a chicken coop. No running water. No electricity. Her life was in trouble, but she faced it the best she could alone.

Her daily routine was extreme. She woke up every day at 2:30 a.m. and hauled her three children down the road to a local gas station. In the filthy bathroom of that convenience store, she bathed her little darlings and prepared them for the day. Then she continued on foot with her babies all the way to a local daycare, where she dropped them off. From there she traipsed off to work at two different waitressing jobs—back-to-back shifts in different restaurants.

With the miniscule amount of money she earned at her jobs, she paid her daycare bill. Daycare was her babies' lifeline. There they had safety, shelter, and food. She would swing by late in the evening, pick up her kids, and take them back to the dilapidated chicken coop. Then at 2:30 the next morning, she would begin the entire process again. That was her existence.

Then, as often happens, she faced a season of sickness, no doubt exacerbated by her personal exhaustion and unhygienic living conditions. When she missed work, she lacked the money she needed to pay for her children's daycare. No daycare would mean no food or shelter for the kids and no babysitters so she could work. Her budget was so tight that the whole process hinged on a mere twenty dollars. Twenty dollars was the price of her babies' survival.

Vera was desperate. She began seeking options, but none presented themselves. Finally she revealed her dilemma to a male "friend." He presented her with an option.

As I pause to reflect on the story as told to me by my foster mother, I realize that my story is exclusively mine. However, its theme encompasses the Tuesdays of millions. It is about identity. *Value*. Ryan did not know his value, and it cost him his life. My millions of daughters across the world are desperate to find their own value because for some cruel reason, no one has bothered to tell them. Naomi certainly did not understand hers at first. I was about to learn the extent of my own.

My mother's friend told her that he would give her the twenty dollars she needed to feed her babies if she would sleep with him. She was desperate. She was needy. She was an easy target. She was trapped by her circumstances, and this low life bottom feeder preyed upon her, exploiting her situation.

She accepted his indecent proposal and slept with him.

So as you can see, I discovered early on what Tuesday is all about. I learned what the world thinks about my value. Though I have never met him, that bottom-feeder was my father. I am the son of a desperate, unwitting prostitute who slept with a selfish man for twenty dollars to feed her babies.

You think you have no worth? My life began at the price of two ten-dollar bills. How's that for value?

My story was beginning to take shape. The truth did not seem very liberating when it first broke down the door of my emotions. It did not thrill me or make me more excited to face the next day. No, it wounded me. However, it was a necessary wound, like an area of the body that has undergone a surgical operation. It hurt, but the hurt was preparing me for healing.

The truth is, *I* needed the truth. The truth is, so do you. Tuesday is the true reality of where we live. Now that you have faced it, there is nowhere to go from here but up. It is time to move on. Let's go there together.

Questions for Individual and Group Reflection

1. Have you ever felt as though your life was the roller-coaster ride that Reggie described in the beginning of this chapter? How so?

_____

_____

2. The search for truth is not a search of creation but one of discovery. How does our discovery of a truth that has always been there create challenges for us? Is truth worth it?

_____

_____

3. What does Reggie mean by "personal Tuesday"? Have you ever had an experience that seemed as if it would never end?

_____

_____

4. How do many people "get off the ride" in the middle of their Tuesdays? What do they miss?

_____

_____

5. What is your impression of Reggie waiting outside Dominic's door? How would lives change if people felt someone was this lovingly dedicated to helping them?

_____

_____

6. Reggie's speech to his "daughters" reveals the needs of a generation. What are these needs? How can they be met?

_____

_____

7. Have you ever known someone whose life seemed like "a pill too hard to swallow"? What do we do when the truth of our lives is this painful?

_____

_____

8. How does the fact that someone is loved bring hope to the truth of his or her reality?

_____

_____

9. What are your reflections concerning Reggie's biological mother's story? Do you see villains in this story?

_____

_____

10. How does truth "prep us for surgery"?

_____

_____

CHAPTER 3

ENGLISH TEACHERS
KNOW YOUR PAIN

THE BEST DAY OF MY LIFE

Childhood is the garden where the seeds of life begin to sprout. It is there that the first seedlings of personality break through the soil, and the world begins to see what kind of plant each of us will become. It is here that we begin to develop our dreams. Our strengths. Our predispositions. Our interests. Our passions. Even our weaknesses. All these things have their origins somewhere in the experiences and perceptions of our infancy, toddlerhood, and adolescence.

I think my brother (my parents' birth son) learned this concept early on. In fact, I remember vividly the day he had a collision with the realities of the world. It was the best day of my life!

He was twelve years old. Twelve-year-old boys live at the intersection of childhood and adulthood. They feel like men in so many ways yet still act like boys in many respects. My brother was a prime example of this strange conglomeration. During the day he paraded himself through school or church as if he were a man. Macho talk. Manly pursuits. Mountain Dew–chugging sessions to impress the girls. He had one hair on his chest . . . and he brushed it every day. You get the point. At night, however, he still enjoyed sleeping in his Batman pajamas. Hence the setting for the greatest day of my life was established.

It was a Sunday morning, and my adoptive mother had already told us to get up and get ready for church. My brother leaned over to me and uttered these fateful words: "I ain't going to church! I'm a man, and I can do whatever I want to do."

I was shocked at his defiance yet strangely entertained by the scenario that was forming before me. So I rose quietly and got ready for church in complete silence, careful not to disturb his manly slumber or the chance of a lifetime to behold the carnage that was surely coming. By the time I was completely ready and standing with bated breath at the door, my dad walked into our room. Seeing me standing there and seeing my brother still snoozing away, my dad had a most confused expression on his face. I filled in the gaps for him.

"He said that he was a man and that he wasn't going to church." Hey, there was no room for loyalty on a day like this; he may have been Batman, but I was no Robin. Against all possible odds Dad actually seemed to increase in size as the anger boiled up within him, beginning in his feet and eventually inflating through his chest and producing a frightening shade of red on his face. The final feature of his werewolf-like transfiguration was a huge vein that popped out in his forehead like a warning shot of his fury to all the foolish trespassers. He looked like a huge Klingon from *Star Trek*, and my man-brother was his pathetic little Tribble prey.

Now if you are of the younger persuasion and are somehow unfamiliar with the original *Star Trek* television show with William Shatner (now, there's a guy who's older than me, whose passion has kept him in show business for decades!—more about passion later) as Captain James T. Kirk, just let Daddy Reggie help you out a bit. Tribbles were cute little pink, fluffy, purring critters from the 1966 sci-fi series. Klingons were their mortal enemies and the show's early villains.

My brother: pathetic little Batman Tribble. Dad: terrifying Klingon. There ya go! Now you're up to speed.

Dad's anger suddenly morphed into an eerie serenity. "He wants to be a man, eh? Fine by me." Then, maintaining quietness so as not to disturb the little sleeping superhero, he scooped him up in his huge arms and carted him off to the car . . . Batman pajamas and all! My brother did not even stir. There he lay, still adorned in his black-and-gray costume. It even had footies!

As we were driving down the road on our way to glory, Batman suddenly woke up. *Bam!* He sat up in the backseat and came to his senses. *Biff!* Looking down at what he was wearing, reality hit him harder than the Joker himself. *Pow!* Suddenly manly-man let out a very girly-girl scream of horror. "*Nooo!*"

My joy was as vast as the open frontier. For support I began singing the Batman theme music. "Na na na na na na na na, Batman!" Umm, if you do not know that particular Batman song from the original television series many years ago, just ask your dad. And do not let him fool you—he *knows* the tune. Obviously I was a great brother. And did I mention that this was the best day of my life?

Batman's panic reached ear-piercing decibels while tears and snot flowed like clear milk and green honey—a pretty poor misrepresentation of Batman if you ask me. He begged and pleaded with Dad to turn the car around and take him back home for clothes, but Dad would not relent.

Finally we could see the driveway of the church ahead of us.

Just before pulling in, much to my chagrin, Dad turned to my brother and said, "Boy, are you going to get up and get ready for church the next time your mother says to?"

A sniffled yes came from Bat Baby.

Then Dad reached under the seat and produced a set of Sunday clothes so he could change. My brother collapsed in emotional relief. And the best day of my life turned out to be short-lived.

BITTER PAIN AND BROKEN PLANES

Bad days . . . really bad days . . . are happening all around us. I am not talking about funny stories with Batman costumes and sibling rivalry; I am speaking of real pain. In the last two chapters we have explored what it means to come to grips with our stories and with the truths found within them. However, just embracing these elements does not yet lead us to the place where we can be mended. Why? It is because these components produce festering wounds that perpetually pulsate with pain. Knowing is not the equivalent of healing.

Pain is the sting with which all people live yet very few individuals ever directly address. Instead, we learn to mask it or compensate for it. We burn bridges and build walls. We allow ourselves to be insulated by pain, guarding our emotional "booboos" like Navy Seals so that no one can ever penetrate our personal fortresses of solitude where our deepest pain is safely secured from would-be intruders.

People's stories and openness to truth will not remove their pain. In fact, removing the pain altogether is not really the goal anyway. Just ask any serious athlete if he or she wants to completely remove the discomfort from working out or playing in games, and a true competitor will tell you that the soreness and difficulty are key parts of an athlete's development. If my muscles did not ache a bit after a tough weight-lifting regimen, then how would I know that my efforts are making a difference? If it were easy to line up opposite a huge running back and take him down with the sheer force of my raw strength, if I did not feel the hit at all, then what would make my tackle anything special? With no pain anyone could play football. No pain, no gain, so to speak. In this respect, pain is an indicator of something. We just have to figure out what.

I can tell you this: if the pain of your past or your present situation is a fixture of your life, if it is a crippling and debilitating feature of your relationships, career, and mental and spiritual health, then you may be aware of it, but you may have yet to figure out the way through it. Notice I said *through* it and not *around* it. I am not here to try to take it all away; no, just as it does for athletes, your pain has value

> **YOUR PAIN HAS VALUE YOU MAY NOT RECOGNIZE.**

you may not recognize. I truly believe it is possible for the pain we each know to be forced to relinquish control of the steering wheel of our lives. It can still ride somewhere in the vehicle, but it is time to change who is behind the wheel.

My life is one of observation. I swim amid the sea of humanity. Young. Old. Broken. Helpless. The prideful who are too full of themselves to even acknowledge their weaknesses. My job takes me all over the globe, so I get to spend a lot of time in airports and on airplanes.

Several years ago I was coming home from a trip to England when, much to my delight, I was unexpectedly bumped up to first class. I sat back in my large, comfy leather chair and antici-pated a long, relaxing flight. What I did not expect was the real-life dramatic production that was about to take center stage right there on that aircraft.

As the flight attendant breezed by, she asked me if I wanted a drink. Diet Coke, baby! It was awesome . . . that is, until a busi-nessman, donned head to toe in his professional garb, sat down across the aisle from me. He loosened his tie and fumbled with his briefcase. His hands seemed to be trembling a bit, and his breathing was audibly heavy. Beads of sweat dotted his forehead. It was obvious to me that something was troubling him.

"Almost miss the flight?" I inquired.

"No, I just hate flying!" he huffed.

I paused to let the obvious sink in even before I said it. "Uh, you're on a plane, dude."

"Yeah, I know. But it doesn't matter because in a few min-utes I'm going to be so drunk that I won't even care anymore."

The same flight attendant came by again, and he grabbed her by the arm. "Bloody Marys . . . three of 'em. And keep 'em coming."

I just shook my head at his antics and repositioned myself for my long respite from the road, but rest just wasn't in the cards. The plane was about to take off when I looked up to see that another flight attendant had sat down in the little seat right across from me. She put her head in her hands. A solitary tear streamed down her face, leaving a black streak of mascara like an emotional breadcrumb trail. She was downcast. The other flight attendant walked over and put her hand on her friend's shoulder. "Are you okay?" she asked.

The distressed flight attendant mouthed the words, "I just

can't live like this anymore." Her friend responded as best she could by offering to do her job for her until we were off the ground and they could talk more. I felt horrible for her but only for a minute because I was distracted by the couple who had boarded the plane and had sat right behind me. My eyelids shot open when the man shouted, "Baby, I love you!"

He was so loud that I wanted to turn around and say, "I love you, too, but I don't really know you."

"Shhh!" the woman hushed. "Whisper, darling."

"I am whispering!" he shouted.

Now, you know that you have a friend like this. You go to the movies. The flick is amazing, so you lean in to your friend and whisper, "This movie is great, isn't it?"

"Yeah, it is!" your pal screams. The entire theater turns and stares at you while an old lady in the second row shakes a crooked finger in your direction and lets out an emphatic "Shhhh!"

Back to the plane. Loud-Talker-Lover-Boy kept spewing his words of undying devotion for all of us to hear while the object of his affection kept trying to quiet him down. Finally he yelled, "No, baby! I don't care if the whole world knows! In fact, when we get back to the States, I'm leaving my wife and moving in with you!"

Again, I could only shake my head. I leaned my head back and came to this conclusion: "This plane is broken!"

I SEE DEAD PEOPLE

I could not take much more, so I closed my eyes and dozed off for a while. When I woke up, it was the middle of the night, and the plane was pitch-black. I decided to watch a movie to get my mind off things. This particular airplane had a very cool movie feature: at the push of a little button on the armrest, a small screen would rise up from below the seat. It was tight!

So I pushed the button. Then I pushed it again. And again. And a few times more. The screen came out and retracted over and over again, and I repeatedly said in my best Captain Kirk voice, "Captain's log . . ."

Eventually I left the screen up and put on my headphones. Across the screen came my favorite actor of all time: Bruce Willis. I was stoked! Bruce was staring with disconcerting wonder at this scrawny little white kid. "Come on, you can tell me anything. Tell me what's wrong."

The boy, eyes wide with horrific reality, looked at Bruce and muttered these bone-chilling words: "I see dead people."

The hairs on the back of my neck stood up. Something was wrong with that kid! I shut the screen and turned on the light above my seat. Shoot, then I turned on all of the lights in my row! But you know how, once you have seen something, it just haunts you to the point that you just have to know? Yeah, that was me. So I pushed the TV button again and watched the rest of the movie. That stinking kid scared me half to death!

Three months later I was on a tour with a Christian musician named Toby McKeehan—known to his fans as TobyMac. These musician guys are like vampires . . . well, minus the bloodsucking part. They stay up all night and sleep all day. So while everyone else would be checking *out* of the hotel at 10:00 a.m., we would be checking *in*. On this day in particular, I went to my room knowing that we had a lot of travel ahead of us and that I needed some sleep. I pulled down all the shades to block out as much light as possible. I turned on the TV just to have some ambient noise, and

I entered that weird state of consciousness where you are gone, but you are not *really* gone. It reminds me of math class when I was in school—the teacher's just droning on, and you can hear her, but your mind is somewhere else altogether.

But then out of nowhere, in the middle of my half-sleep, a familiar voice rang out: "I see dead people." I jumped up out of bed certain that the little white kid was somewhere in that room, and he was after me! Darting toward the window in a desperate attempt to let in some light, I tripped over my suitcase and fell forward, grabbing the curtain and pulling it completely off the wall and on top of me.

There I lay, in my underwear, wrapped up in humiliation and a filthy hotel curtain, staring aimlessly up at the popcorn ceiling. Then I heard, "Own this movie on DVD today." That's when it hit me. I thought back three months earlier to that jacked-up plane ride, and I realized that I see dead people all the time:

The man who cannot control his drinking. I see dead people.
The woman who just cannot take another day of her life. I see dead people.
The man who is throwing away his family. I see dead people.
Kids at local high schools. People in airports. Everywhere. I see dead people.

STRETCH IT OUT

Pain is an itchy security blanket. Over time we become accustomed to it even though it is uncomfortable and makes us scratch. Yet we need it, and soon we wrap ourselves up in it so that the *real* us is unreachable beneath the layers of pain. That exterior cover is what we usually encounter with people—the story that encapsulates their lives with hurt and regret. Thus, we see their pain, but we seldom get to meet the actual person underneath. Many choose to stay bundled up like emotional Eskimos.

> PAIN IS AN ITCHY SECURITY BLANKET. OVER TIME, WE BECOME ACCUSTOMED TO IT, EVEN THOUGH IT IS UNCOMFORTABLE AND MAKES US SCRATCH.

My favorite book tells a true story of a guy who went to a religious meeting one day while hiding some crazy real pain. He had a withered, deformed hand. No doubt he probably tucked that hand away under a cloak or inside his clothes so that he would not draw attention to himself. But what he did not know was that on that day he would be unexpectedly and unequivocally challenged to stretch out that which was most obviously the source of his life's anguish.

My favorite character in that book was also in that room that day. Against all conventional logic of the culture of his day, he called for the man with the withered hand to stand up in front of everyone. He called him out! Can you imagine already living with the stigma of a deformity in a society where those with physical or mental special needs were considered to be outcasts, and then having someone call you out to stand up in the middle of a crowded room? That guy must have been terrified, but it was only going to get worse . . . or better, depending on how you look at it.

After the man was standing there in front of everyone, no doubt hiding his deformity as best he could, the hero of the story spoke yet again: "Stretch out your hand." Now if he was anything like me, he probably stretched out his good hand first. Why? Because we don't want to expose our pain. Our humiliation. Our heartache. Our weakness. Our shame. We do not want anyone to see what we are hiding beneath our emotional and spiritual cloaks. Just let us blend in and live with it, but do not tell us to stretch it out into the light where it can be seen.

> WE MUST BE WILLING TO STRETCH IT OUT. STRETCH OUT OUR TEARS. STRETCH OUT OUR FEARS . . . STRETCH OUT OUR LIVES.

But that is exactly what he was told to do, and that is exactly what he did. You see, in order to experience the mending of our wounds—the realignment of that which is dislocated, the reanimation of that which is disheveled and completely destroyed—if we are to experience this kind of life-altering, world-shifting change, we must be willing to stretch it out. Stretch out our tears. Stretch out our fears. Stretch out our insecurities. Stretch out our weaknesses. Stretch out our lives.

So what happened to the guy with the shriveled-up hand? We will come back to him.

BACK TO SCHOOL

Calling people to "stretch it out" is what I do all over the world. I walk into schools and call out students and teachers alike. What a rush it is! It is like drive-by loving. When they get up, brush their teeth, copy their friend's homework assignment on the school bus, and get yelled at by their homeroom teacher, they have no idea what's coming at them. They are clueless that they are going to be paraded into a crowded room where a big ole black guy named Reggie is going to call them out and challenge them to stretch out that mess they have been hiding away all these years.

Don't worry; I'm gentle with them. I am not out to embarrass anyone. In fact, the only person I really ever make fun of is me. If you have ever seen me, then you understand. I am no stranger to pain or having everyone stare at me. You do not go through life looking as I do and miss out on what it means to be made fun of and teased.

Growing up, the only things I heard more than the internal voices reminding me that my mom did not want me and that I would never know my real father were Fat Albert references. Yeah, I know a little something about stretching out your pain.

The kids of this world need to know that everyone

has something to stretch out. Parents. Pastors. Politicians. Teachers. Especially teachers. That is why when I speak at a school assembly, I almost always have the teachers join me up front to do some goofy dance or to rap in the microphone. You have not lived until you have heard a football coach from an all-white Appalachian school in the hills of East Tennessee try to throw down a phat rhyme in the microphone in front of the whole school. Oh yeah, I make 'em stretch it out there.

At the end of the day and at the end of our lives, we just want to know that we are not alone. My goal is to get this message to people before the ends of their lives precede the ends of their days. I have actually met students who were planning suicide the day they attended one of our assemblies, only to have someone ask them to *stretch it out* for the first time. Abuse. Neglect. Rejection. Addiction. The names are many, and the pain is more widespread than any flu epidemic in this world.

But I know, and you do as well, that this particular sickness is not quarantined within the confines of the public school systems in our world. Every member of humanity is infected. Every one of us bears the scars of old wounds or the open lacerations of life's fresh lesions. When it comes down to it, we all need to go back to school in the sense that we all need someone to call us out and challenge us to stretch out that which seems most vulnerable and painful.

Stretching it out is an action that few individuals in this world are willing to take. We are too young to care about issues better left for a later time in life. We are too old to rehash the past and dredge up feelings and emotions that time should have healed by now but hasn't. We are too cool or influential, whichever label best fits your generation, to allow others to know what lies hidden beneath the Batman costume we are secretly wearing. So we slumber away in the most covert form of pride that exists: the arrogance that says, "I'm too far gone [or too private or too weak or too embarrassed or too scared] for anything good to happen."

The only problem is, what remains unrevealed also remains unhealed.

ENGLISH TEACHERS

As you may have gathered, sometimes I think teachers are as affected by our public assemblies as the students. Who could blame them? Who else has such a front-row seat to the carnage of adolescence parading through our school systems—hormonal bulls in the china shops of young lives? So I love getting teachers to stand up in front of students and get a little crazy. Oh yeah, they know they are most definitely not being laughed *with*;

it is a blatant moment of being laughed *at*. But that is exactly what everyone in the room needs: more laughter. Laughter does more than simply trigger some internal emotion of humor; it cleanses the entire emotional palate and creates the potential for other emotions to be dipped into as well. Have you ever laughed so hard that you cried? There you go.

Toward the end of my presentations, I always ask for the hands of all the English teachers in the room. Considering the usual spectacle I have just made with the other teachers and administrators, it is a wonder that they dare to raise their hands at all. Fret not, though, because you can always count on students to throw their teachers under the proverbial bus and brazenly point them out like a Las Vegas neon arrow on the Strip.

Why choose English teachers specifically? To answer that question we will need to pick up my story as I left it in the last chapter. As I told you, I am the product of a twenty-dollar sex agreement. Bluntly stated, my mother sold her body to a sexual predator because it was all she knew to do. But don't feel sorry for me because I promise you that I am worth more than twenty dollars!

Some time passed in our home after my foster mom enlightened me about my biological mother's history. After a few years I became curious and inquisitive about what my biological mother looked like. Momma pulled me onto the couch and took out an old school yearbook. Turning to a page with a bent corner—a telltale sign that she had been there many times before—she showed me an old classroom picture. The students in the picture were second graders, little kids all lined up in rows.

Standing beside them was a beautiful woman. "Who's that lady, Reggie?" my mother inquired in the sweet voice that was hers alone.

"That's you, Momma!" I replied. "You're so pretty."

"Thank you, baby, and that's right. That's me as a second-grade teacher." Then she pointed out a little girl in the second row and told me to remember her face. Reaching for another, bigger yearbook, she again turned instantly past pages that had felt her fingers many times over. She stopped on another classroom photograph, tenth graders this time. A slightly older yet still equally beautiful lady was standing beside the class.

"Momma, that's you again!"

"That's right, baby."

Are you starting to put it all together?

Momma then moved her finger to one of the girls in the class. "And that is your mother. She was one of my students in second grade, the one I showed you in the other picture. Then she was my student again in my tenth-grade English class. I was your mother's English teacher."

Momma went on to tell me the story. When the little girl was in second grade, my mom told all of her students that if they ever needed anything at all, they should call her. Imagine the young lady's surprise when she walked into her first day of tenth grade and reencountered her beloved childhood elementary teacher. By this time Vera already had her first child, Keith. She and Momma reconnected. And as she had done in second grade, my mom again offered to help Vera with anything she needed.

What that gracious English teacher could not know were the mistakes and abandonment that Vera would face soon after their fateful reconnection: a second pregnancy and her parents splitting town, leaving her with nothing; a deserted high school dropout, she tries to raise three babies in a halfway house; a tragic move to survive leads them to living in a chicken coop; and a twenty-dollar proposal results in another pregnancy.

The pressure was just too much to bear, and Vera simply had nowhere else to turn. One night the phone rang at Mrs. Dabbs's home, and on the other end was a desperate young woman, her former student. My mom and dad came to her rescue. They moved Vera and her children into their home and took care of the little family for the duration of Vera's pregnancy, literally saving their lives.

When the time came for the little bundle of joy to be born, Vera knew she could not handle another child in her already complicated life. So right there at the University of Tennessee

Medical Center in Knoxville, she unexpectedly turned to the only person in all her life who had ever cared about her or had ever attempted to show her real love, and she made the greatest request that could ever be made of anyone on the planet. She asked my mom to raise me as her own child. My mom said yes.

When it was all said and done, by the age of eighteen, Vera would have four children in three years. When I was born, she gave me up. I temporarily became a ward of the state—my birth certificate actually says "Property of the State of Tennessee." Mr. and Mrs. Dabbs immediately took the necessary steps to become my foster parents and, eventually, my adoptive parents. In fact, they were the ones who brought me home from the hospital. They became my family.

So that is why I have a soft spot for English teachers. Trust me; it is not because of my grammar!

People have different reactions to this story and different viewpoints about my biological mother. Some think she abandoned me and that her poor decisions were inexcusable. She definitely made some doozies in her life, but all I know is that I would not be here today without at least one of those decisions. She is a testament to the hope that can emerge out of hopeless situations. What should have been a closed-door case and a wasted life on the identical path of my biological parents has instead become a story of hope for millions of people all over the world. It is not a perfect story but a story of redemption. I do not say this to boast or brag about myself. Come on, man! I am here because a young girl was so distraught that she would do anything to survive. I have nothing to brag about except the change that has occurred in my life.

Many people want to know what happened to my biological mother. Truth be told, I have never met her in person. I was told that she married and kept her other three children. I have often wondered about my siblings, but I have never tried to contact them, and they have never contacted me. Honestly, I have always felt that if contact were ever made, it would probably have to come from them.

When I did meet my mother on the phone, it was not under the greatest of circumstances. The first time we ever talked was when my adoptive mother passed away, much later in my adult life. Vera called to express her sympathy. These days she calls periodically to say hi, which is a whole lot more than many children out there can say. Is my family story a source of pain in my life? Sure, but it is a pain that has been healed and has purpose.

Pain can have purpose? Sure it can. If we go back in time, that young, misguided unwed mother made one key decision that has changed the lives of countless people: when it counted, she stretched it out. You can call it abandonment or weakness. Or you can call it the ultimate surrender, and surrender is scary no matter the situation. Yes, she made a host of poor decisions. If we were being honest, we would admit that most of us have made our fair share as well. We can't change the past, but we can take action in the present and change the future.

Remember the guy with the withered hand? He stretched it out, and when he left the building that day, he had two good hands with which to embrace his new life. Though I have never met my mother, I am thankful that she placed her young boy in a home where he would be raised in love and have all he needed to survive and even succeed in life.

Your story may not be as extreme as my biological mother's or even mine, but you do have something that needs to be surrendered, some issue that needs to be stretched out. As we continue this journey, we will talk about the process that takes place after you put that pain out there; but for now, do you have the courage to take off your Batman mask and come clean with what is hidden under your sleeve?

The man with the Bloody Marys. The husband about to leave his family for another woman. The flight attendant who just could not take another day of living. I see dead people. Maybe when you look in the mirror, you see dead people, too, but the good news is, we do not have to stay dead unless we want to.

Questions for Individual and Group Reflection

1. Have you ever had an experience like Reggie's brother's Batman-pajama incident in which your decisions almost cost you dearly? Explain.

   _____

   _____

2. How is pain the insulation of our lives? How do we use it to try to keep people from hurting us even more?

   _____

   _____

3. What observations did you make about the three different people on Reggie's first-class flight experience? Their circumstances were unique, but what did they have in common?

   _____

   _____

4. Do you see "dead people" around you in your life? How so?

   _____

   _____

5. How can pain become our "itchy security blanket"? Why do we hide that which causes us the most pain?

   _____

   _____

6. What emotions do you think the man with the withered hand must have felt when he was told to "stretch out" his hand?

_____

_____

7. Reggie said, "What remains unrevealed also remains unhealed." Do you agree or disagree with this statement? Why or why not?

_____

_____

8. Why do you think Reggie pulls teachers into his school presentations? What effect do you think this has on the students?

_____

_____

9. What did the fact that Reggie's adopted mother was his real mother's teacher reveal about his adopted mother's heart for her students? Do you know anyone who has this kind of heart?

_____

_____

10. We can't change our past, but we can take action to address the pain that was caused then. What pain from your past needs to be "stretched out"?

_____

_____

CHAPTER 4

BUS STOPS AND BATMAN
KNOW YOUR HERO

SHOCKED BY THE TRUTH

As a result of the time I spent in foster care, I was granted the privilege of knowing what it felt like to have a family. However, family is not always what it's cracked up to be, especially when your older brother turns out to be Satan himself. I know, I know, you are wondering how and why Satan would choose a quaint little house in Knoxville, Tennessee, as his chief place of residence. Believe me, I have contemplated that question for more days in my life than I care to reveal. But just know this: Satan had a nickname—Kenneth.

At first glance my older adoptive brother, Kenneth, passed the basic litmus tests of brotherhood. We lived in the same house. We both called the same two people Mom and Dad. We even shared (by the sheer forceful will of our mother) toys, clothes, and the occasional ice-cream sandwich. Yet beneath the deceitful skin of my sibling lay the secret identity of Lucifer himself. How do I know? Simply put, he often tried to kill me.

Examples? One will be enough. Picture a pristine fall day when the leaves are just getting crunchy, yet they still glow with the colored brilliance of their autumn beauty. After some time playing in the yard, Kenneth and I found ourselves inside the house and, for some reason, standing in the bathroom. A young and innocent lad of only six or seven years old, I had become increasingly inquisitive and foolishly trustworthy all at the same time. Hey, come on—if you cannot trust your brother, then whom can you trust?

As we were playing, a question suddenly loomed in my psyche and broke through the barrier of my lips. "Hey, what's behind those holes that makes things work?" The holes in question were the electrical outlets. Here I was, just little Reggie trying to make it in the world, minding my own business, yet innocently seeking the answers to life's hardest questions, especially that elusive explanation as to why plugging and unplugging items from those holes was the key to whether or not things worked. Did Kenneth see fit to answer my question? Indeed he did.

Leaving the room for a moment, he returned with a metal clothes hanger. Unwinding it in his hands, he gave it to me, saying ever so convincingly, "Here, put this end of the hanger in one hole and this end in the other. Then you'll know what's behind those holes."

With naïveté smeared across my sweet little face, I took the hanger in my hands, oblivious to the danger that would follow.

Pmmmph! The whole house went dark. Somehow, I was teleported to the other side of the bathroom. I regained consciousness amidst a cloud of smoke rising from the smokestack of my Afro.

That was Kenneth. *My personal devil.* Nevertheless, he was my brother, and though much pain was inflicted upon me at his hand, everyone knows that big brothers are heroes to little brothers. He may have picked on me in ways that folklore could not exaggerate, but I pitied the fools who would have tried it themselves. When it came down to it, I knew that he was a hero of mine—a really strange hero, who often tried to destroy me. But he was not *really* Satan, I don't think.

BUS STOP BLUES

I was so blessed to have my family. Yes, even Kenneth. I can only imagine what my life would have devolved into without the benevolent and undeserved love of that overly kind tenth-grade English teacher. However, despite the love I was given, the knowledge of my story and the shame of it all still managed to seep into my bones. I felt alone. Abandoned. Unworthy of love. I knew my story, my truth, and my pain. But knowing these things was not enough; I needed a hero.

No single moment brought these emotions to the forefront more than a fateful day at a bus stop. I was ten years old. My routine for going to school went something like this: I would catch the city bus and ride into downtown Knoxville. After getting off at the bus stop situated amidst the big buildings and businesses, I would walk to another bus stop in order to catch the school bus.

On that day in particular I was not paying attention and carelessly bumped into a tall gentleman. He was dressed in a business suit. In my mind he was larger than life itself. I could only imagine what kind of office he must have been heading to and what kinds of world-changing business he must have had to conduct. I bet his briefcase housed important documents, and he had a secretary who handled his calls and made his lunch reservations.

The kicker was his Caramello-like skin tone, just like mine. After I bumped into him, he patted me on the head and kindly said, "Excuse me, son."

Son? It had been two years since my mom had told me the truth about my mother, and from that day forth, I had felt somewhat alone. Destitute. Desperate. I was a castaway on a deserted island where even my own father and mother had no interest in finding me. Somewhere out there, I knew my father existed. I had been looking for him intently. Could this be . . . could it be . . . could he be the one I had been seeking?

> I WAS A CASTAWAY ON A DESERTED ISLAND WHERE EVEN MY OWN FATHER AND MOTHER HAD NO INTEREST IN FINDING ME.

The kind man walked away; I followed after him. I did not think about my bus. I did not think about my foster parents. I did not think about anything in the world except to wonder if that man was my dad. I could not let him out of my sight. He turned onto another sidewalk perpendicular to the street we were traveling. I turned in tow. He made another turn. Left this time. I was his shadow, yet he never saw me, at least that I could tell.

Finally he came upon a large professional building and scaled the front steps, opening the huge glass door at the entrance, and disappearing into another world that felt so far away from any world I thought I would ever know. I stood outside that building and stared the best I could through its tinted glass front, trying desperately to distinguish the reflections from the actual silhouettes within. He was gone, and I stood frozen, as if my feet had been placed into blocks of wet concrete and had hardened. It was a heartless mob hit to my soul, and I sank fast into the cold, somber deep.

From the depths bubbled an isolated thought I had often felt but never faced head-on . . . until then. It was a voice—an unwelcome one—and it told me, loud and clear: *You are alone. Completely. Utterly. Totally alone.*

WORTH THE WEIGHT

I have never forgotten how I felt that day. The aloneness tattooed me somewhere down deep inside. That's what pain does—it brings definition to our stories. The thing is, though, that we have choices as to how this pain will shape us.

Consider for a moment that we are standing in front of a weight bench, and the barbell is loaded with two forty-five-pound weights on each side. For many people that is pretty heavy. But heavy means different things for different people. For one, the weight means danger. If you are goofing around with the weights while someone is walking past, the weights could shift and fall, maiming or even killing that person. The media was riddled recently with a story of a college athlete whose hands slipped off the barbell while lifting. The weight he was attempting to push up vertically came crashing down, instead, on his neck. Narrowly dodging death, he required surgery and a massive amount of recovery time to get out of the woods.

Weight means something else for the one who prepares himself to lift it properly. Stretching. Starting out with manageable amounts and building up to the bigger stuff. Pacing. Hydrating. Breathing properly. Being spotted. Being cautious. Through this process, the same weight that can kill the careless lifter can make the deliberate one stronger. Same weight, different results.

Pain is a weight that each of us must approach in our own way. Your weight bench will not look like mine, and mine will not look like yours. Yours may hold depression, anxiety, drug abuse, sexual addiction, insecurity, doubt, crippling fear. The weights are daunting, yet we each must walk into the pain room. The choice that we have, however, is whether our weight becomes the thing that crushes us or the very thing that builds our muscles into strong solidity. The decision belongs to each of us individually.

Pain is the common denominator of humanity. It cannot be reduced by mathematical deduction. It does not disappear just because we ignore it. It is there—the weight in the room where we live. Our options are either to position ourselves under our pain and begin lifting like the dickens to build the strength we have yet to feel or to let the weight crush us into powder. Still breathing but not really living.

WEIGHT LIFTING WITH SUPERHEROES

This is where heroes and villains are born. Often, when I am speaking in public school assemblies, I will verbally poll the students in order to ascertain their favorite superhero. I give them four choices: Superman, Batman, Spider-Man, or Iron Man. If you had asked me this question when I was in middle school or high school, I would have most definitely picked Superman. Indestructible. Incorruptible. And he gets to wear his underwear on the outside of his pants! Come to think of it, that part's pretty weird.

The crowd is usually torn. Superman, Batman, and Spider-Man all get a smattering of applause. They are the classic heroes, our childhood heroes. They continue to be reinvented in the modern media by huge movie productions that glisten and dazzle with the kinds of special effects that I only dreamed about as a kid. Back then, we actually had to use our imaginations. Go figure.

Each hero has his own set of strengths and weaknesses. As I said, Superman would appear to be the hands-down choice, but I think his little underwear problem scares a few fans away.

Batman, at first glance, seems to really have the stuff of heroes. However, a closer examination reveals a startling truth: Batman is really just a brother with a tool belt! I mean, come on—he does not have any real super*powers*; he just has super *toys*.

Spider-Man. Now, there's a character! A geek turned hero. I can really relate to that. His story is riddled with pain and misunderstanding, yet one little bite on his hand from a radioactive spider and—voilà! He is shooting webs out his wrists.

Oddly enough, the recent crowd favorite has overwhelmingly been Iron Man. For us classic hero guys, Iron Man does not seem like the first choice. But this generation loves him, mainly because of Robert Downey Jr.'s recent bad-boy portrayal of Iron Man in the box-office-hit movies. Kids like what they have most recently seen.

In some ways Iron Man is a lot like Batman—he is a rich dude with some crazy toys. His only difference, though, is that his heart is so injured that he has to connect it to something greater than himself in order to survive and to do something worthwhile in this world. Ooh, now, that's nice!

In fact, when you really break it down, that is the typical story of every superhero. *Pain that leads to choice that leads to action*. Superman is an orphan on a planet full of people who are nothing like him and do not understand him. He must keep his identity hidden, which means no one can ever truly know him.

Spider-Man is also an orphan. Loved by some and hated by others, he is a freak of nature, tormented by his own poor choices that cost his uncle's life. He lives in pursuit of redemption. His identity hidden, he must wear a mask to protect people from the truth of who he really is.

Iron Man has to almost lose his life in order to become

something bigger than he is. Every battle for him is an issue of the *heart*.

Batman witnesses the massacre of his own parents and spends the rest of his life wrestling with the demons of fear and bitterness that drive him to take action against injustice. Again, another story of pain, another mask, another hidden identity, and another hero is born! For a moment, let's take a closer look at Batman.

DARK NIGHTS FOR THE DARK KNIGHT

One of the most recent superhero movies to turn the heads of our culture is *The Dark Knight*. Besides the incredibly cool gadgets and the memorable chase and fight scenes (and the always entertaining Morgan Freeman), there is a thematic thread weaving its way through the story of Batman and his nemesis, the Joker. One is a hero; the other is a villain. The uncanny truth of their respective existences lies in the fact that they have similarities that cannot be ignored. Both have experienced violent childhood trauma. Both live with personal vendettas and wrongs that they seek to avenge. Both, by their own admission, live a little on the east side of sanity, if you know what I mean.

That is the difference maker between epic heroes and diabolical villains: they each respond to the weight of pain in different ways. One decides to rise above it and use that pain to strengthen himself, while the other slithers beneath it and uses it as the excuse to avoid the good of life. *One pain; two choices.*

When I stood outside that professional building and felt the dagger of the reality of my pain, I had a choice. Society would say I did not have a choice, that I was destined—even doomed—to falter beneath the weight of my parents' poor choices. According to every conceivable expectation my world had for me, I was made to be a villain, foreordained to spend my life leeching off those I deemed entitled. Fated to ignore my conscience until its calluses had completed their nerve block on my feelings and I felt nothing but the inward thirst to look out solely for my own interests. I should have been a druggie. A womanizer. A have-not. A high school dropout. A taker.

Within the dramatic evolution of the Batman saga is the appearance of a third character, Harvey Dent. At first the newly appointed district attorney is the personification of all that is just and right in Gotham City. Bent on righting society's wrongs and punishing those responsible for them, Harvey seems to live above the psychological issues of Batman and the Joker . . . that is, until the weight of pain deals him its crushing blow.

After the death of his fiancée and a life-altering injury that chars the entire left side of his face, Harvey is no longer the noble guardian he once was. He feels an aloneness with which my ten-year-old bus-stop self could sympathize. Everything changes for him. His pain begins to eat away more than the skin on his face; it also eats away his choice, or at least he thinks it does.

Harvey—or Two-Face, as he eventually becomes known—sets out to exact vengeance on those he deems responsible for his pain. Moving from person to person in a torrential downpour of violence, he repeatedly allows their fates to be decided by all that he thinks is left in life: chance. The flip of a coin. Heads, they live. Tails, they die.

This chance-versus-choice paradigm becomes a key concept in the story. Two-Face is convinced that chance is all that is left in life because of the pain that seems to randomly fall like an anvil on unassuming and undeserving bystanders. That is where many of us end up. We decide that life has already dealt us a losing hand, so we might as well leave the outcome of the game to chance. Besides, we have no choices anyway.

But there is a crucial truth to be learned. Two-Face's seemingly just method of leaving life's fate to chance—refusing to choose boldly the outcome *for himself*—was actually a choice in and of itself. And the same is true for us. To avoid choice is to make one: the choice of avoidance. It is a choice to accept the sentence of pain—to willingly succumb to the crushing weight instead of trying again to lift it.

Those who do not choose to be a hero choose to be a villain. The Joker convinced Two-Face that he could live by chance and still find justice, but in following the Joker's advice, Two-Face became the very villain he had fought so hard to vanquish. It was the weighty context of his pain that flipped the switch and sent him into his tailspin.

That is who we are: Harvey Dents who have two faces. One is the noble face of a hero; the other is marred and wrecked with pain and bitterness. Both Batman and the Joker beckon us to embrace our destinies as heroes or villains, but the Joker's argument is different. He promises a compromise. He vows that the fence is rideable and can be successfully straddled. He tells us that we can leave things to chance and still somehow stumble across our inner hero.

> TO AVOID CHOICE IS TO MAKE ONE: THE CHOICE OF AVOIDANCE. THOSE WHO DO NOT CHOOSE TO BE A HERO CHOOSE TO BE A VILLAIN.

> *WILL YOU BE THE PROBLEM, OR WILL YOU BE THE ANSWER? WILL YOU SAVE THE DAY OR DESTROY IT?*

Those who listen to the Joker and elect to leave their lives to chance are actually and sometimes inadvertently making the choice to become villains. Inaction is action. To avoid a choice is to make one. Standing alone outside that building in Knoxville, I had a choice, and I knew it. I decided that the utter desolation of aloneness I was feeling was something I never wanted anyone else to feel. Yes, the pain was heavy, but I would rather lift it than be crushed by it. Of course, I did not make this conscious decision at age ten, but I did decide I did not want the pain to beat me. I made up my mind that choices for me did exist.

What sentence has been read over you? Are you "destined" to be a failure? A loser? An outcast? A poor student? A bad parent? An unfaithful spouse? Does the die seem already cast? Are you stuck with the chance happening of poor luck—someone with no real choices in life except to become exactly what the cards of life have dealt you?

That was me. That is you. But you know what? The morphing into hero or villain is a choice we each make for ourselves. Will you be the problem, or will you be the answer? Will you save the day or destroy it?

DEFINING MOMENTS

I never quite shook that bus-stop experience. The feeling that I was alone, that so many other people were completely alone, played in my mind over and over like a constant movie score. I could not shake it. I knew that I did not want to be the villain, but indeed it seemed to be my fate.

The next part of my story is both the moment of definition of my life and the moment of definition for this book. What I am going to share will be the very piece of information that will cause you either to shut this book and roll your eyes or to reevaluate your own viewpoints concerning the journey of a hero. Please know that my purpose is not to speak what you are expecting; neither is it to shove my own experience down your throat. I do not seek to prove truth; I simply seek to shine the light on my story and the stories of thousands of others out there so that what is true will become easily visible.

It had been two years since my fruitless sidewalk episode after the man I had hoped was my father, and I was in a church service with my mother and father, doing all the things that most twelve-year-olds do in church. Doodling. Daydreaming. Drooling. Yet on this day the preacher's topic piqued my interest in the most peculiar way. He was talking about love.

Crucial sidebar. I beg you not to fit my story into the preexisting schematic you already have in your mind about church and religion. If you immediately smell the mothballs of your grandmother's living room where you used to gather after church, if you hear boring and poorly played organ music accompanying even stuffier lyrics written in some form of ancient English that is foreign to you, if you remember a teacher or a preacher or a misguided parishioner smacking the tops of your hands with rulers or browbeating you into a terrified state of faux repentance, then yeah, I am talking to you. You are the one who stands to lose the most from my story because you cannot help but humanly cram my experience into your own mental compartments. You may think, *I went to church my whole life! I know what goes on there! I know how fake and hypocritical those holier-than-thou people are! Don't talk to me about church, Reggie! Go sell your "crazy" somewhere else because we're all full here!*

If this is your reasoning, then you have the potential for your moment already to have been defined. If you so choose, the past, the pain, or the ineffective efforts of well-meaning people can define your moment. It is like reading a Microsoft Word document you saved some two years ago in a read-only format. Staring at mistakes and issues that need correction, you are stuck, and the system will not allow you to make or save any changes. In other words, church or spirituality can become a perpetual list of uncorrectable mistakes if you let it.

It is time to hit "Save As" and change the name of your experience from "My Reality" to "My History." Oh, what a huge difference there is between our history and our reality. When we allow our history to be our only reality, we get perpetually stuck in the land of villains. We lose the present and inadvertently create a future we would never desire. We cannot write new paragraphs in the story. We are stuck reading and rereading the same old messed-up narrative.

> WHEN WE ALLOW OUR HISTORY TO BE OUR ONLY REALITY, WE GET PERPETUALLY STUCK IN THE LAND OF VILLAINS.

What I am saying is, before you make your decision about the story you *think* I am about to tell you, try letting my chronicle be stored in some part of your inner cosmos that stands on its own. In other words, your negative experience with spiritual matters does not necessarily mean that spiritual matters are all negative any more than a road full of bad drivers means that all cars are evil: "Hey, this road is full of horrible drivers! I'm through with cars!" Today is a new day, so don't make lump-sum assumptions. Let my story stand or fall on its own.

Back to the church those many years ago. I put aside my fidgetiness and began to listen as the man on the stage spoke of love and acceptance. These were topics I had heard of and had indeed experienced through the gracious actions of my adoptive parents. However, that large hole within me was still gaping with emptiness. The rejection and shame of who I was and where I came from taunted me. It was like being at a huge meal yet lacking the sense of taste. You are eating, yet you cannot comprehend what is going into your mouth. I knew my adoptive parents loved me, but their love just could not fill my void. I needed to taste it for myself.

Out of nowhere the speaker seemed to change his tone, looking directly at me. "You! Jesus loves you!"

"Me?" I exclaimed out loud in adolescent wonder, involuntarily rotating the heads of the entire front section of the church in my direction. Momma grabbed my hand and told me to hush up. What she had not seen was that the man was speaking directly to me.

He made his way over to our pew and said, "Son, what is your name?"

"Reggie."

A Grand Canyon–sized smile broke out across his face. He looked deeply into my eyes and uttered words that literally changed the reality of my present and the direction of my future by adding a new chapter to the shame of my past.

"Yes! Jesus loves *Reggie*."

You may think a twelve-year-old was an easy target. You may think I was so desperate for love and acceptance that any declaration of the sort would have sent me down an idealistic path of faith that would coax me into some well-wishing existence of false redemption.

The fact is, though, no matter what you may think, you weren't there. When that man told me Jesus loved me, something happened inside of me. It was internal. Eternal. Paternal. I had heard my whole life that Jesus loved me, yet that was the first time it was spoken somewhere louder than my ears could hear. *Louder than my past. Louder than my pain. Louder than the Joker's voice telling me I was destined for the life of a villain.* I heard it somewhere deep inside. And you know what? It took!

I made a choice that day, mainly because I found out that Jesus had already chosen me. Me! A hopeless, hapless, helpless son of a young, unwed mother so desperate to survive that a one-time offer of prostitution from a selfish villain was all the hope she could see. Jesus had chosen to love me, and I realized that if I chose to accept that love, I would never again stand alone outside the walls of my father, longing to get in. I would have a Father about whom I would never have to wonder. His identity became clear that day. He was not ashamed to call me *son*. He was not far away; he was speaking directly into my heart.

I listened. I responded. I found my hero, and I entered the quest to become a hero too. I vowed that, through the reality of love I had experienced in God, my life would be dedicated to helping the other orphans of this world find that same love.

I don't know about you, but being Two-Face is not the life I desire. Leaving life to chance and denying the existence of our choices only lead us to places we do not want to go. You know, we may not become diabolical or destructive, but when we are hurting, our lives can definitely become wrapped up in self-absorption and pettiness. *And self-absorption leads to selfish actions.*

Like Harvey Dent, each of us bears two faces. Two sides of a coin. Two directions that pull at us. We are stuck between the affections and dreams of a hero and the bitter hopelessness of a villain. We must choose.

The truth is, God has already chosen you. You may not believe that, but the fact that you are reading this book is another extension of God's hand toward you. He sees your pain, and he is not denying it. He feels it!

The ultimate hero is the one who lays down his life for others. Forget which compartment in your brain religious-sounding statements may currently fit into, and let this simple yet profound truth ring in fresh ears: how much Jesus must love you if he was willing to die in your place before you had ever heard of him or asked for his help. What kind of crazy love is that?

It is a love that redeems you from your past. A love that frees you from your guilt, leads you through your weakness, and gives hope to the blank pages in your story ahead. It's a love that brings Truth to your truth, hope to your story, and perspective and healing to your pain.

Villain or hero? The choice is yours. How do you choose to be the hero? Easy. Ask Jesus to be the hero in your life. Believe that he died for you. Believe that he came back to life for you. Ask him to forgive you and set you on the hero's path. Hand the weight of your pain over to him. Suit up for greatness by putting on his strength and forgiveness. Be a weight lifter instead of a punching bag.

I certainly don't want to come off as cliché or pseudo-religious. Instead, I think I will just be real with you. I am the last person on the planet who should be speaking truth into anyone else's life. When you strip away all the details and put things into simple terms, all the good . . . all the hope . . . all that truly matters in my life is a direct result of the moment I met Jesus. He became my personal friend—my personal hero. You don't have to believe my words; the change in my life is undeniable.

My hero already knows you well. Your name. Your situation. Your hesitation to move. Maybe, like me, your complete feelings of abandonment and shame. Your seemingly inoperable pain. Your doubts that he even exists. Your suspicion that his followers are simply well-wishing, and you are their next coin to be tossed into the depths of blind faith.

I think what most people do not know is that the hero *knows*. We think he is aloof. Uninterested. Disappointed at best. But what if the only real, legitimate reason we feel this way about him is the simple fact that we have never actually met him personally? You may have met the hypocrisy of certain people who advertise his name on their building or marquee. You may have met *religion*, but if you have not actually met *God*—himself—for yourself, then how can you ever really know?

> SUIT UP FOR GREATNESS BY PUTTING ON HIS STRENGTH AND FORGIVENESS. BE A WEIGHT LIFTER INSTEAD OF A PUNCHING BAG.

If God is truly unknowable, then you have nothing to lose. Ah, but what if he is the hero you need? What if he is more than you expect? If so, then it might be time to destroy whatever negatives about him exist in the musty darkroom of your mind and open your heart's door to the illuminated possibility of a real experience with him.

It may seem odd to you, but that spiritual doorknob can turn right here in the midst of this book. It can go down like this: if you have already met him personally, then close this book temporarily and spend a few minutes with him. Just because you have met him does not mean the process of knowing him has ceased. Revisit your own hero story with him.

If you have never met God, I would like to make the personal introduction. I have no magic words. I have nothing that can change you. He is the one who will take care of all the details. What I want to do is lead you into an encounter with him. I could call it a prayer, but most people have preconceived notions about prayer. Prayer really just means communication with God. I also do not want you to think *my* prayer is the key. What is important is that you open up your heart and mind, that you surrender all the good and bad—that you make yourself available to know him as deeply as he already knows you.

That conversation with him could look something like this (pray this with me if you are ready):

Jesus, if you're "knowable," then I want to know you. I want to be washed clean from all the things that could separate me from walking with you. Please forgive me. I thank you for inviting me into your life; now I invite you into mine as well. I believe you died for me and that you came back to life for me so that I can be alive, both now and forever. My heart is open to you, and I thank you for coming in and making yourself at home in me. My future may be uncertain, but I'm ready for my relationship with you to be sure and steady.

I love you, God! Thank you for loving me! In Jesus' name, amen.

I truly hope you decided to give my hero the chance to do in you what he has done in me. Meeting him is just the beginning; now it is time to get to know him. The truly thrilling part is that knowing him is never fully complete because there is an infinite amount of him to know. Like any great love story, there are always more chapters to write. In other words, this is not a one-time meeting; this is a lifetime seeking. So let's keep walking and find out what new adventures lie just around the next bend of life's pages.

Questions for Individual and Group Reflection

1. Considering the "shocking" story of Reggie and his brother, can you think of any childhood stories of foul play among you and your siblings or friends?

   _____

   _____

2. What were your impressions of Reggie's bus-stop experience? What did it reveal about his desire to be loved by his father?

   _____

   _____

3. How far are people willing to go to find love?

   _____

   _____

4. How does pain "tattoo" us somewhere deep inside? How does it bring definition to our stories?

   _____

   _____

5. How can "weight" mean two different things to different people?

   _____

   _____

6. Who is your favorite superhero? What are the tragic features of his or her story?

_____

_____

7. In what ways are we like Harvey Dent? What can happen to us when we live life according to chance instead of choice? Do we become heroes or villains? Explain.

_____

_____

8. How is the avoidance of choice actually a choice itself? Explain.

_____

_____

9. How do our past experiences and preexisting notions of religion affect our perceptions of spiritual things?

_____

_____

10. What do we have to lose by genuinely asking God to be our hero? If he is not real, then what will be the harm? If he _is_ real, then what will be the gain?

_____

_____

CHAPTER 5

OLD-SCHOOL PEAS
KNOW YOUR CHOICE

OLD SCHOOL

These days, there are all kinds of styles of parenting and family communication. Some parents seem to have adopted a negotiation method with their children. Let's take a look at this new-school scenario as it plays out in an average household.

A conscientious mother works busily in the kitchen, trying to get the whole family ready for their day. Down the hallway, a sixteen-year-old is getting dressed for school . . . boy or girl, it really does not matter. The stage is set. Mom calls down the hall, "Sweetie, do you want cereal or eggs for breakfast?"

"Neither! I don't want any breakfast!"

Hmmm. Now, that is an interesting response. The evolved, negotiating parent might reply with something like, "Okay, sweetie. I understand if you don't want to eat this morning. I'll just put some extra money in your bank account today so you can use your debit card if you get hungry later on. Is that okay?"

"Whatever." Ah, the typical reply.

That is what I would call *new school*. However, I did not come from a new-school household. In my house, we were definitely kickin' it old school. Let's replay the previous conversation through an old-school filter.

"Sweetie, do you want cereal or eggs for breakfast?"

"Neither! I don't want any breakfast!"

Hmmm, now, that is an interesting response. The antiquated yet effective old-school parent leaves the kitchen and makes her way to the room of the sharp-tongued teen. The door is closed. Inside, the unassuming adolescent readies himself in his natural habitat. The right shoes. The right jeans. The right hairstyle. Everything must be perfect, "or else I will just *die* when I get to school!"

The teen hears a mysterious rumble in the distance. The surface of the water in the glass on the dresser begins to ripple in short intervals in true *Jurassic Park* fashion. The teen begins to sweat a bit but is unsure why.

Suddenly the door bursts open from the brunt of the foot of the old-school parent. With wild eyes flaming with the fury of a thousand burning suns, she enters the room with a frying pan in one hand and a spoon in the other. The teen's focus suddenly shifts from fashion and the upcoming social cares of the day to sheer survival. Unlike the new-school kid, the old-school kid frantically searches the recesses of the mind in an attempt to recall what heinous thing was said that initiated this grim sequence of events. All the while, saying nothing, the parent continues a snail-paced approach toward the teen. No words are necessary; the frying pan and spoon say it all.

The frying pan . . . the spoon . . . that's it! thinks the sweaty student. "Mom, what I meant to say was, 'I would greatly appreciate cereal this morning, if that's okay with you.'"

The mother stops, eyes still locked in on the target in soldieresque focus. She lacks any real expression. But then, a small smile suddenly makes an appearance on her previously stoic facial contours, just enough of a smile to unnerve the kid. Raising her eyebrows and becoming eerily chirpy, she replies with, "Okay, sweetie! Cereal it is!" Then she turns and leaves the room. The teen lets out a sigh of relief.

Yeah, that's old school!

OLD-SCHOOL PIGGIES

I was definitely raised in the old-school style of household communication. I was not really afraid of losing my PlayStation 3 or getting grounded from texting. I never worried that Mom or Dad would delete my Facebook profile. Nope. I worried more about things like never again seeing the light of day or walking with a limp.

Okay, in all seriousness, my parents would have never done anything to actually harm me. They loved me. They taught me that I had choices and that I was responsible for what I did with those choices. You can call that old school if you want; I call it love.

I remember this lesson really hitting home when I was in the third grade. Our schoolteacher had just sat the entire class on the rug for reading time. The story of choice that day? *The Three Little Pigs.* What a classic! I had already heard this one from my parents at home.

My teacher (we will call her Miss Piggy) began the story, and everything was great until she got to the part where the first little pig, who had unwisely built his house out of straw and had it blown down by the big bad wolf, fled to the second little pig's house. I piped in with, "Nuh-uh! That's not how it happened!"

> *MY PARENTS TAUGHT ME THAT I HAD CHOICES AND I WAS RESPONSIBLE FOR WHAT I DID WITH THOSE CHOICES. YOU CAN CALL THAT OLD SCHOOL IF YOU WANT; I CALL IT LOVE.*

The teacher paused and looked at me. "Um, yes, Reggie. That is how the story goes."

"No way!" I insisted. "That piggy's dead!"

A collective gasp arose from the third graders around me. I was killing more than just that pig; I was killing their innocence.

"Reggie, now that's enough! Why would you say something like that?"

"He's dead! My daddy told me so!" I was emphatic, and there would be no changing of my determined little mind that day.

After school, the teacher called my dad and asked him why I would say such a thing. Dad came back with, "Yeah, I told him that pig died!"

The teacher was appalled. "But why, Mr. Dabbs? That's not how the story goes."

"That's how it goes in this house, and I'll tell you why. I don't want my boy thinking that he can just continually do what is wrong and get away with it every time. Sometimes, there won't be another house to run to when you don't acknowledge the consequences of repeated wrong choices. Sometimes, your choices can get you eaten by that wolf."

His point was made, and so is mine. We were old school; but in today's world, old school has come to mean something completely different. People frown on the idea of such rigidity in thought. They prefer to act as if it does not matter what kind of "house" they build in this life because there will always be another place to run to. They dodge personal responsibility as if *it* is the wolf that is out to eat us.

Don't get me wrong. I live my life telling people all over this spinning globe about the second chances that are available to them. For that matter, I tell them about the millions of chances they have to become heroes in their futures, but that does not mean they should not strive to make the right choices in the present.

The promise of forgiveness was never meant to be a license to deliberately and cold-heartedly continue to live a lifestyle that will require forgiveness with no change of heart. That sort of change is not new school; it is *no* school. An experience of faith that does not change motives and actions is nothing more than a meaningless moment of emotion.

Once we have known the hero without, who is working to produce a hero within, we can truly begin to understand the power of our choices and the freedom we have to choose what is best.

BEACHSIDE BUILDING

How do you change your future? You do it by building the house of your present life upon the right foundation and by using the right materials. Call it old school if you want, but the truth will never change: your life is the sum of your choices. Sure, we all start with our own unique set of circumstances. Some are born into riches; others open their eyes in squalor. Some have natural athletic abilities while others can barely walk a straight line without stumbling. We may all approach the game of life with different circumstances, but we each possess one characteristic that spans all people of all nations and of all situations: choice.

My favorite book tells a story about this very concept of choosing the foundation upon which we will build our lives. It says that the wise man built his house on a rock. In today's terms that is the equivalent of pouring a solid concrete foundation before building. It just makes sense.

But the wise man had a neighbor who decided to build his house on the lot next door. This man is given the name *Foolish*. Nice. How would you like to carry that name all through high school? "Hey, Foolish! Give me your lunch money, or I'll beat the snot out of you!" Okay, so maybe that was not his actual name, but that was definitely his title. In all fairness that title was not just bestowed upon him. No, he earned it by his choices. He chose to construct his own house upon nothing but sand (Matt. 7:24–27).

Notice the significance of the story, that the man used sand versus dirt. A house built on dirt in one of the Plains states might actually stand for some time. Eventually it would begin to settle, and there would be structural problems. But for a while it would be okay.

But if Foolish built on the sand, that indicates these houses may have been located near a coastal area—they were probably beach houses. If you have ever been to the beach, then you know that houses there are much more likely to experience strong storms, high winds, hurricanes, and flooding. Things get easily lost in the sand because the nature of sand is to shift under the power of the elements. If you have ever laid your keys down next to your beach towel, then you know how sand can seemingly swallow things up in an instant.

So the dude built his house on the sand. What does *house* represent here? His house represents his life. Our houses are the places where we feel secure. We bring our families under their roofs and lock their doors for safety. We spend our time mowing our lawns, painting walls, and cleaning floors because our houses are where we live. They are where our most valuable possessions are located and are often hidden in undetectable nooks, crannies, and crevices. We decorate the walls with pictures of memories past and invite our closest friends to visit. Our houses are extensions of ourselves.

You probably know the rest of the story as well as you know the one about those three little pigs. No surprise here, but a huge storm hit both houses. Well, yeah! They were on the beach. The house on the rock stood firm, sustaining a few cosmetic injuries to the siding and roof.

Casa de la Sand? Not so much. It was completely demolished by the gale-force winds. And you know what probably happened? The owner and builder of that house probably stood outside the rubble, scratching his head, thinking, *Hmmm. Now, I had no idea that a storm would come right here on the beach. I really thought it was always sunny around here.*

Storms hit everyone—that is the constant. Hard times. Depression. Sickness. Rejection. Confusion. Abandonment. Everybody deals with some form of hurricane-force hardship. What will vary are the choices individual builders make in the construction of their lives near the common beach of trouble. We all know that the winds are coming, yet we will not all choose to find a rock upon which to build.

It is not what comes at us that defines us; it is what we do with what comes at us. Rock or sand. Hero or villain. Old school or new school. Choice or chance. Significance or selfishness. The choice is mine; the choice is yours.

HEY, HEY, HEY!

The choice I made to answer Jesus' offer to know real love changed everything for me. It may have been my most significant choice in life, but it definitely was not the last significant choice I would have before me. Choosing to follow after God actually creates a series of other choices to consider. The path of a person of faith is not a cruise-controlled life with Jesus "taking the wheel" in a way that would make Carrie Underwood proud. You may love that song, and I agree that it is great and all, but if you ever actually start spinning on a sheet of black ice, whatever you do, do not "throw your hands up in the air." Instead, just pray while you continue to steer. It doesn't make for a good country song, but it makes for good survival.

I was a twelve-year-old who had just answered God's loving call, and I had a new lease on life. However, the necessity of making choices continued. I decided that since I finally had the thirst within me quenched by the love of God, it was time to tell others about my new favorite drink. The memory of standing alone outside that office building collided with the reality that God would never leave me alone and my desire that no one should ever feel what I had felt, and it led me to dedicate my life to helping others find what I had found.

When I reached high school, I took on two paper routes. One was for my own financial needs. The other? I worked the other route to raise money to sponsor my friends so they could attend a

Christian youth camp that was coming up that summer. When it was all said and done, five of my friends attended, and every single one of them left that camp at the end of the week with a new relationship with God. To be honest, having this kind of influence—positively affecting the lives of others and being a hero—was almost intoxicating. I knew right then I wanted to spend the rest of

Photo courtesy of Linda Forsee

my life helping other people realize they have choices and that through God they could choose a life of significance and purpose.

But it was not easy, not in the least. I was still a huge black kid who stuck out like a sore thumb. Despite the fact that I had found purpose in my life, my high school years were still riddled with difficulty. For starters, I was torn between football and band. On the one hand, football was the choice of athletes. It was a surefire way to ensure avoiding the bullies. Besides, I was pretty good at it. The band? Not so much for the bully avoidance. Truth be told, though, I loved music.

My love of music was instilled in me by my mother, who insisted that every one of her children play an instrument. I wanted to play the tuba, but my mom made me play the saxophone instead. Saxophone—I hated it at first. As it turned out, though, I was a natural. I could play anything I heard, even songs on the radio.

By the time high school hit, I was a man torn between two

> TO BE HONEST, HAVING THIS KIND OF INFLUENCE—POSITIVELY AFFECTING THE LIVES OF OTHERS AND BEING A HERO—WAS ALMOST INTOXICATING.

worlds. I was a social half-breed of sorts. The football players made fun of me because I was in the band, and the band members resented me because I played football. I did not know whether I should *be* the bully or *run* from the bullies.

Another key reason for many of my hardships had to do with a little cartoon that came out when I was in school: *Fat Albert.* If you are too young to have seen the show, try Googling it, and you will get the picture. You can imagine. I learned just how cruel high school could be. If I heard "Hey, hey, hey" once, I heard it a million times. Oh yeah, that is just what every high school kid wants—every person in the hallway comparing you to a dude whose first name is Fat. Let's just say I was not exactly teeming with self-confidence.

A PEA-SIZED HERO

My favorite book tells a story of another man who lacked self-esteem. If you have not figured it out yet, that favorite book I keep referring to is the Bible. Now, before you freak out on me about how boring the Bible is or how it does not relate to real life today, just know that Reggie does not spend all of his time reading. I'll tell you more about that later. Trust me, I am no bookworm. So for me to say that the Bible is my favorite book is really saying something. I only say it because the Bible completely changed (and is continuing to change) my outlook on life and, particularly, my life itself. Need an example? Try this one.

Just as I lacked self-confidence in high school, there was a man you can read about in the Bible who also did not fit the hero's mold. His name was Shammah.

For as long as anyone can remember, most men have been defined by what they *do*. Doctors. Lawyers. Athletes. Pharmacists. Bus drivers. Garbage men. I guarantee that as you read that list, each job conjured up an image in your mind. It does not necessarily make you judgmental; it just makes you human. For the most part society is bent on defining us by what we *do* in this world.

Let me tell you. Shammah had a very special job. He was a farmer. I am not digging on farmers, but most of us do not expect crazy heroics from average farmers. But it gets better. The crop that he cultivated and produced was lentils. In other words, he was a pea farmer. Put that on your résumé for greatness: "Well, just before I became the president of the United States, I raised peas out in my field."

Could it be that Shammah was just like you or me? He may have lacked self-confidence. He may not have understood his own potential. Maybe he sat up late at night, staring at the stars above and feeling miniscule beneath them. What difference can a pea farmer make in such a great big world?

Just as they did on yours truly, people looked down on Shammah. He probably faced ridicule and tomfoolery on all fronts. Sometimes the impressions others have of us can leave quite a bad taste in our mouths—the bitter tastes of worthlessness and insignificance. While others are reaching for their dreams, we are stuck here in the pea patch.

Shammah had more than just bullies to worry about; he had enemies. His enemies were a neighboring nation of Israel called the Philistines. If you are new to the Bible, just think of the Philistines as the ultimate diabolical villain against Israel. Israel was a nation God had set apart for his own purposes. They were destined to be heroes. However, enemies like the Philistines continually threatened to destroy them. Not that they needed any help in the destruction arena. The Israelites were usually in trouble more for their own stupid decisions than they were for anything else.

It was during one of these *troubled* times when Israel had walked away from God that Shammah found himself in the predicament of constantly being raided by the Philistines. Apparently the Philistines loved peas. Pea soup. Pea casserole. Pea pie. Dried peas. Peas in a blanket. You get the point. That made Shammah an easy target. He could not count the number of times the Philistine raiders had swooped down and stolen the peas right out from under his nose.

Can you imagine his frustration and shame? Months of digging and planting and fertilizing and weeding and watering, all wasted in a matter of minutes. I can just see it now: Thirty or forty Philistine warriors appearing over the horizon. Shirtless and sporting six-pack abs that rivaled any Spartan from the movie *300*, sweaty and hungry for their favorite pea recipe, riding valiant steeds foaming at the mouth (the steeds, I mean), and swords drawn to intimidate any of the little pathetic pea farmers in their way.

Shammah was weary, tired of cowering down to the

muscle-bound enemy. Tired of losing everything he had worked so hard to grow. Tired of having to explain to his wife and kids why there would be no peas again this year. Tired of not fighting back and making a stand for what mattered to him.

Finally the tiredness within him turned to resolution. Something snapped in Shammah, and it was not the peas. Pulling the shovel out of the ground next to him, he did something the Philistine raiders were not expecting. Instead of running away from them, he ran toward them. Dwarfing any Mel Gibson *Braveheart* battle cry, Shammah let out a spine-shivering scream that halted the unsuspecting warriors in their tracks: "No!"

Picture it: Forty or so of them on horseback, armed with swords. Here comes one crazy pea farmer with a shovel. Laughter must have broken out from across the field. But Shammah was *not* laughing, and he was *not* running away this time. He had had enough, and he was not willing to lose one more pea to his enemies.

Before they knew it, Shanghai Shammah was on them. Double flipping over the first horse, he knocked its rider to the ground. The next one went down just as easily. Soon the chorus to the song "Kung Fu Fighting" was heard in the background as Shammah cracked skulls and scattered the confidence and bodies of his attackers. He even pulled off a midair, slow-motion, *Matrix*-style body bend that ended in a roundhouse kick. When the dust cleared, Shammah had killed every single Philistine who had come to steal his peas that day.

Needless to say, the Philistines avoided his field in the future.

IMPASSIONED AND EMPOWERED

I have felt Shammah's pain. I know what it feels like to be close to snapping. My high school years in Knoxville were filled with Philistine raiders. They came after what was important to me—my confidence, my self-worth, my security.

The raiders were not all just bullies and mean kids. Sometimes the enemies rode the horses of my own thoughts, galloping into my head and taunting me with my own shameful history. They reminded me of what I could not do and how my life was nothing more than a pathetic pea patch. I would never amount to anything. I was worthless. What I did on the football field was not enough to earn me acceptance. What I could do with a saxophone was not enough to find significance. Many mornings found my pillow soaked with the tears of the previous night. I had found meaning in life, but I was still under constant siege.

It is important to note that Shammah did not simply just get mad one day. No, something else happened within him that was bigger than a glorified temper tantrum. Shammah became impassioned and empowered. The impassioned part dealt with his mind and heart. He suddenly became aware that the time for hiding out and taking the beating from the Philistines was over. His peas may not have been much, but they represented his life's work. His family. His nation. His God. In the end they were symbols of what was important to him.

Second, God had empowered him to do something that no normal pea farmer could have done. Make no mistake. It takes an act of God to take out forty armed men with the swoop of one's shovel. Shammah was more than just a bad dude; he was a dude empowered by a powerful God.

Fulton High School was my pea field. It was there I first began to learn the extent of my enemies' attacks upon the very lentils of my existence. If I did not fight back, then I would spend the rest of my life hiding out like a coward. Everything I would plant or work for in life would come to nothing. It would be stolen away, and I would watch it ride off into the sunset.

My breaking point was not a physical reaction to a physical bully; it was a spiritual reaction. I decided to let the millions of tears I had shed become fuel in the tank of my dreams. I became impassioned to see the value of the peas in my field. My dreams. My friends. Even the strangers walking past me in school. I was not going to take it anymore. It was time to stand up and fight. It was time to be empowered to do more than the world thought I could do. It was time to reach my breaking point.

> I DECIDED TO LET THE MILLIONS OF TEARS I HAD SHED BECOME FUEL IN THE TANK OF MY DREAMS.

I was not perfect. I made many mistakes, but I fought hard. I spent my entire high school career trying to make a physical and spiritual difference in the lives of all those around me. I prayed publicly in the locker room and in the band room. I never touched alcohol or drugs. I began to take myself *less* seriously and God *more* seriously.

Once a boy threw out the old familiar, "Hey, hey, hey" in my direction.

I fired back with, "Hey, at least I got a cartoon! What you got?"

I became bold. I became impassioned. I became empowered.

By my junior year people were well acquainted with my faith

and what I stood for. One day two absolutely huge brothers who played on the football team with me cornered me after practice. I was bold, but I was not above being scared to death by the prospect of getting clobbered by a couple of Goliath-sized linemen. They told me I was coming with them after school. Wisely, I did not resist.

We left the school and walked up the hilly street to the hospital located just west of the school. When we walked in the door, I asked my new friends what was going on. They informed me that their mother was dying of cancer and I was the only person they knew who prayed. Whether I wanted to or not, I was going to be praying for their mom to be healed.

I prayed. Today, some twenty-five years later, their mom is still alive, and both of those guys know God in a personal way. That was when my faith completely collided with my life—and I liked it! I wanted it to be that way in everything I did. If the Philistines were going to come, they were going to have to defeat

me to get to what was important to me.

I suppose that is why high schools are so important to who I am today. They take me back to a time in life when I became impassioned to take my pea patch personally. It was there that my faith turned me into a fighter. It was in those difficult times that I learned I was way stronger than I first

Photo courtesy of Linda Forsee

realized and that God was way stronger in me than I had ever imagined.

Most days I return to the scene of my own pea field incident—public schools. I see Shammahs in all walks of high school life. They are freshmen. Seniors. Tough guys. Sweet girls. They are abandoned. Hopeless. Plundered. And scared.

But you know what? They are my peas, and I will fight for them. I know the sting of living with no hope, and I found out that I could win impossible battles if I was just willing to be broken. My breaking point was the turning point in my life.

High school shaped me, and it still shapes me today. Nothing thrills me more than watching God use my impassioned and seemingly powerless self to empower a generation of students with a message of strength and love found in the midst of weakness and hate. Simply put, God's choice gave me my choice. I did not make all of the right choices, but I did choose to be who I know I am supposed to be, independent of everyone else's opinions and actions. My response became my responsibility, and I took ownership of it.

If you and I want to truly know the path that has been laid out for us, we must know that we own the power of choice, and we must embrace it as the power to choose the right actions and reactions in life. We must choose to fight for our personal peas.

Questions for Individual and Group Reflection

1. How do you relate to the "old school" and "new school" scenarios at the beginning of the chapter? Which scenario best fits your experience?

   _____

   _____

2. What were your impressions of Reggie's adopted dad's version of *The Three Little Pigs?* Do most people truly understand the power of their choices?

   _____

   _____

3. "Life is the sum of one's choices." Do you agree or disagree with this statement? Why or why not?

   _____

   _____

4. The equalizing factor of the house-building story was the storm. Do we live our lives as if we expect the storms? How would our choices change if we did?

   _____

   _____

5. Why is choosing to follow God not the last choice we will ever make? What other choices does this choice produce?

   _____

   _____

6. As a pea farmer, Shammah did not seem qualified to be a hero, yet he made choices that set him apart as one. What choices did he make?

_____

_____

7. Why were his choices not enough? What was the "God part" that empowered his choices and routed his enemies?

_____

_____

8. What things make you feel impassioned? About what things do you think God wants you to be impassioned?

_____

_____

9. Why is it crucial that God's empowerment accompany our passion? What can happen if we are simply passionate without power?

_____

_____

10. The power of choice is the power to choose both our actions and our reactions. What are the differences between the two?

_____

_____

CHAPTER 6

PINKY-TOE IMPORTANCE
KNOW YOUR VOICE

A BODY DIVIDED

The little things matter. Little strides make a marathon. Little days make a lifetime. Little is big.

You don't believe me? Try not listening to one of the littlest parts of your life: your little pinky toe. Ah, yes, the pinky toe. It is the last toe located on the outside of your foot. It is the fifth toe—unless you're from Alabama, where it might be your sixth. Ha! Just messin' with you!

Little pinky toe. Come on, we don't even know why he's there. Tiny toe with even tinier toenail. Insignificant. Not crucial to anything worthwhile in life. You could probably live without him, right? We don't have to listen to old pinky, do we?

You decide. It was 3:29 a.m. From a dead slumber my eyelids shot open like spring-loaded window shades. Three hours earlier, I had made the inauspicious decision to chug two entire liters of Diet Coke, thinking that it would not faze me. Oh yeah, I was fazed. My brain, the boss of this old body of mine, sent a message down the various corridors of my body's inner communication system: "We got to go . . . now!"

The rest of my body agreed wholeheartedly. The hands were fine with the decision. My nose could not care less. The eyes piped in with, "Fine by us. Let's all just go, and we won't even open. Brain up there knows exactly how to get there without our help. We're going to just keep on sleeping." Even the internal organs, such as the spleen and pancreas, were in agreement with the brain's directive. This body was getting up and going to the bathroom. The kidneys and the bladder began to plan an elaborate tickertape parade in the brain's honor.

But as the body-wide (I said *body-wide*, not *wide body*) conversation escalated to a dull roar, a tiny voice rang out from among the chatter: "No!" it squeaked. "Please don't do it! Not again!"

"Did you hear something?" said the solar plexus.

"Nah, that was just the floor creaking," replied the kneecap.

"I'm not the floor, you morons! I'm down here at the bottom! You're not listening to me."

The left eye rolled his . . . well, himself, and said, "Oh, that's just pinky toe."

"Pinky toe?" A collective groan rose from the entire body.

"Shut up, Pinky!" screamed the brain. "This is an emergency!"

Pinky piped up. "No! I won't be quiet! I remember what happened last time, and I just now regrew my nail. If we're going to the bathroom, you tell those stupid eyes to wake up, or else I'm not going!"

Laughter ensued. "Pinky, you can't stop us! You're just the stinkin' runt." The colon was relentless.

"Hey, Colon, you're the one that's stinkin'! Why don't you try a little cleansing every once in a while?" Pinky may have been small, but he was a spunky little appendage. "Look, guys, none of you seems to remember or care about what happened the last time we tried this. It's just a bad idea, and if you're wrong, I'm the one who's going to suffer."

Brain had heard enough. "Look, this is happening, so everybody needs to just suck it up!"

Pinky continued to protest, but his sentiments fell on deaf ears, and other body parts as well.

The body . . . my body . . . began its nocturnal journey to accomplish the mission at hand. Brain did the driving. "Okay, guys, easy breezy. The door is right here; I'm certain of it." The only problem was, the door was not exactly where Brain thought it was. "Right foot, swing out," directed the confident Brain.

Right foot went out, and *pmmmph!* It crashed into the doorframe. Pinky toe's worst nightmare came to fruition. As it turns out, somebody should have listened to his little voice. I screamed and fell to the floor in agony. Oh, if only my brain had listened to that seemingly insignificant little pinky toe. If only.

THE POWER OF ONE VOICE

In high school I felt like the pinky toe. The idea that I would grow up to speak to millions of students each year in high schools all over the world would have been completely crazy. I was a horrible student. I struggled with all things academic. Yet, somehow, I managed to walk across the stage of my high school in cap and gown. From there I decided it was time to try my luck in college.

My freshman year found me struggling through grueling classes at the University of Tennessee in Knoxville. I knew early on that I was in way over my head. College for me was more of a concept than a reality. I grew up as a huge Tennessee Volunteers fan. I loved watching the great Reggie White crush his offensive opponents. I loved the history, and I loved to deck myself out in orange and white and scream, "Rocky Top!" at the top of my lungs.

What I did not love so much about Tennessee was going to class. I did not love chemistry. I did not love studying. As it turns out, my classes didn't love me either, as was evidenced by a dismal GPA. So the following year—at the advice of some amazing friends, Pastor Don Wilburn and his wife, Janice—I transferred to Evangel University in Springfield, Missouri. I relished my two years at Evangel. Epic pranks that I cannot mention here. Pillow fights that left people unconscious. I made many friendships that have lasted a lifetime, and I learned a lot about ministry, which was great but still did not translate into better grades. I still struggled immensely with all things academic. My GPA continued to plummet, and I knew at that rate I would never graduate. I needed a change of direction. I needed help.

I was on a five-year path to an undergraduate degree *before* the five-year path was common. I would like to think I was ahead of the cultural game, but that was not the case. Anywho, the summer after my second year at Evangel found me licking my wounds at a job several hours from home. I worked on staff at a summer camp called Camp Ambassador in Goodlettsville, Tennessee, just outside of Nashville. It was there the course of my future was altered.

Camp was seven incredible weeks of hot days, late nights, and messy games. As a staff worker my days included everything from preparing and serving food in the kitchen to putting Band-Aids on minor boo-boos in the nurse's station to cleaning toilets in the bathhouse. The only thing worse than the hours was the

pay, but I relished every minute of it. Working at camp was
an experience that shaped my
work ethic and my impres-
sions of the value of ministry
to youth.

Camp had multiple focuses.
One focus was obviously to create an environment for kids to
have the time of their lives. You
have not lived until you have
taken every single leftover food
from an entire week of camp,
mixed it in with gelatin and a

Photo courtesy of Linda Forsee

healthy dose of curdled milk, set it out in the sun for four or five
hours, and then poured it down the face of an unsuspecting youth.
Hey, what's a little vomit among friends?

The other key spotlight of the camping experience was spiritual growth. Camp Ambassador was one of the places where I
had some of the most significant encounters with God of my
entire life. These days, the camp goes by the name of Camp
Jackson. Time would not permit me to tell of the thousands of
students since the 1960s who found faith or deeper measures of
it in those woods. A week away from technology's distractions
and, in many cases, time away from the horrors of neglect and
abuse back home, combined with the energy of thousands of
other kids whose hearts are all open to God, is sometimes just
the catalyst needed to see a young life changed forever.

If that's what happens in one week, imagine being there
for an entire summer. Don't get me wrong; it was hard work.

But amid the work was an introduction that set me on that new course. One week the camp speaker was a gentleman named Rick Olsen. Rick was a college professor in speech communication at North Central Bible College (now North Central University) in Minneapolis, Minnesota, and was also an experienced speaker in the public schools. That week at camp, his style, delivery, and genuine concern for students captured my interest and catapulted my imagination concerning the impact one voice can have on the lives of individuals.

Besides his skill as a speaker, he was very personable. As a young man still feeling my way through the rigors of college and career, I found his kindness and his general demeanor magnetic. I thought he was cool, but apparently he saw something in me as well. We became friends that week, and that is when he made a *little* suggestion that started my brain thinking in new directions. He invited me to come and visit the school where he taught.

To be honest I had never heard of North Central, much less considered applying there. But Rick made such an impact in my life that week that I thought to myself that if any college had a professor as cool and as real as he was, then that was where I wanted to go. No college visit. No preplanning. I applied, got accepted, and moved to Minneapolis that fall. That was that.

I did not really realize it at the time, but Rick was a huge example of the power of one voice to change the direction of a life. His one voice gave me the courage to leave behind my beloved East Tennessee—and the campus in Missouri I had become so well acquainted with—and venture into lands unknown to the sole inhabitant of Reggiedom.

ATTENTION AND DEFICITS

I have already shared briefly with you about my academic struggles. Sometimes I think I was the dumbest brother on the face of the planet. I had problems thinking clearly and staying focused. As a football player and band member in high school, I found ways to navigate my way through the easier curriculum. College, however, was an ADD kid's worst possible nightmare.

My new alma mater and my change of geography did not produce any new abilities to excel as a student. College became a battle—no, scratch that. It was an all-out war that rivaled any gruesome Mel Gibson battle scene in history. My enemy was not the faculty or professors, although sometimes I would have loved to roll their cars in Saran Wrap. I was not fighting against the bullies of high school anymore. No one was deliberately trying to trip me up. No, my enemy was my own personal academic weakness. I was the cause of the battle.

It is hard to fight against yourself—to look in the mirror and see your opponent. To be both your own protagonist and antagonist at the same time is a huge challenge. Over time you begin to hate yourself; maybe you can sympathize. It would be so much easier to pick out some nameless, faceless jerk out there who is setting out to derail you, then stick out your chest in defiance to stand up to him. *To finally get fed up.* But what do you do when you are fed up with . . . well, yourself? Now that's tough.

Every graded paper that had a D or worse written at the top of the page was a constant red reminder of my ineptitude. With each failure, another piece of my dream was fading away, hopelessly sucked into some all-consuming wormhole of ignorance that I could not escape. Failure was a tractor beam that had me

> IT IS HARD TO
> FIGHT AGAINST
> YOURSELF—TO
> LOOK IN THE
> MIRROR AND SEE
> YOUR OPPONENT.

well contained within its gravitational pull.

Once again I was in over my head; there was no doubt about it. Not only was I aware of it, but so were the people around me. At first they did not vocalize their concerns, probably out of some hopefulness that the switch would flip on one day, and I would *get it*, whatever that means. It never happened, and I kept spiraling downward. My confidence and self-worth took new adult-sized nosedives into waters I never knew in adolescence or high school. I had survived the perils of being a screwed-up kid only to get to college and become a screwed-up young adult.

Attention Deficit Disorder (ADD) is a widespread problem in our culture. Theories abound about the cause of this epidemic of unfocused behavior. Some think it has to do with the amazingly scattered nature of our entertainment and technology. We go from one television show to the next with a bombardment of fast-moving commercials demanding our attention in between. We ride in cars with radios blaring, cell phones in use, video games being played, and DVD players showing us movies we have usually seen a thousand times already. We have trouble focusing because a million things in our lives are all demanding our attention.

Others think that the problem stems from our lifestyles. From an early age, most kids these days are shuffled from school to soccer to band to church to homework and then to bed, with no chance to breathe in between. We have become obsessively active. Holidays used to literally mean "holy days," sacred days when we rested and reflected on life and living. Now we work ourselves into such a froth that we eventually collapse into momentary lapses in the madness—we call them vacations. Literally, we feel the need to run away from our crazy lives to find any respite—to *vacate* life as we know it. No wonder so many kids and adults struggle to find focus in their lives. Which of the two thousand things, each screaming for our undivided attention, are we supposed to focus on?

I am not exactly sure what caused my attention problems, but they definitely caused deficits in my life. Deficits in my grades. Deficits in my time. Deficits in my self-worth. No one wants to feel like an idiot, but it is hard to deny it when the world keeps shouting that you are. My world screamed at me for the first two years of college, and the deficits seemed irreparable.

A ROYAL SCREWUP

As it turns out, I was not the first human in world history to deal with Titanic-sized deficits. Just consider Moses. For most people the first thing that jumps out at them about Moses is not that he was a screwup. We think of terms like *prophet, leader,* or *miracle worker.* In all actuality, though, Moses was a *royal* screwup in every sense of the word.

His childhood story started out pretty badly. Here was this abnormally beautiful child born into a poor family that was part of a whole race of slaves in Egypt. *Strike one.* (You look good, but no one respects you. Ah, it's a sting I know well.)

Next, the crazy pharaoh got his proverbial royal pants in a wad and went loco on all the Hebrews. Get this: he sent out an order to kill all of the male children under the age of two because he feared the size and power of the Hebrew nation. Killed thousands of innocent children? He was one messed-up dude! Moses was doomed from the start. Again, I can relate.

His mother, desperate to save her little boy from the edge of the Egyptian's sword, made a waterproof basket and placed him in it. Then she floated the basket out into the Nile River and put Moses's big sister, Miriam, on watch to make sure nothing happened to him. (Older siblings watching after us? Need I remind you of my older brother, Kenneth, and the hanger-in-the-outlet debacle, as it came to be known?)

Again, the little floating pretty boy seemed doomed. But against all odds Moses managed to emerge from muddy waters and somehow stay clean, this time literally. Pharaoh's own daughter found the little picnic basket while bathing in the river and discovered that there was no peanut butter and jelly sandwich inside. He melted her heart with his cuteness, and she decided to take him into her own family—to adopt him into royalty. Wow! Things were finally looking up for old Mo.

With an incredible stroke of divine fortune, Moses's real mother was chosen to care for him while he was a baby. However, the day finally came when Moses matured to the point that it was time to move into the palace with his adopted mother, the princess. It was a crazy day for a little slave boy. From rags to riches. From dirt floors to marble hallways. From making bricks to the study of the arts and playing sports. Things really seemed to be looking up for Mo Mo (let's keep adapting his nicknames as we move forward . . . just go with it).

But, just like yours truly, Mo could not seem to shake something that followed him everywhere he went. Nothing was wrong with his life; no, he was the most privileged Hebrew in all of Egyptian history since the days of his ancestor Joseph. He had beaten his old life, but it just seemed as if it would not go away. All he had to do was what the Egyptians were doing, and he would have been fine. Study. Eat. Learn. Flourish. Rule.

Instead, anger welled up within him to the point that he murdered an Egyptian. Oh, what a difference a few days can make! One day Mo was dining on the culinary delights of the most advanced civilization in history to that point, lounging on silk sheets, and taking dips in the private royal riverfront pool of the Nile—possibly the same pool where his adopted mom had found him. Fast-forward a couple of fateful hours and Mo was crawling through a desert on the brink of death from dehydration. He had had it all; he had been given so much. Yet he just could not shake . . . himself.

That is what it feels like to live in deficit. Mo and me would have been bros! Two brothers from multiple mothers. And so he found himself far away from home on the backside of the desert, herding sheep on a mountain. I bet that more than once he sat down on a dirty boulder and contemplated what the stink was wrong with him. *Dude, all you had to do was shut up and live! Now you're scooping up sheep poop in the badlands. What a waste!*

I was scooping up my own version of poop in Minnesota, the badlands compared to my beloved Smoky Mountains. Sorry, Minnesotans, you know I love you! But just as it came for Moses, a day was coming when I would have to make a decision to either lose my way forever, by finally accepting the seemingly unchangeable sentence of my own deficits, or face up to who I was and fight for the future I knew I was supposed to possess. Taking no action would have been an action itself.

But how is a "brotha" supposed to go from ADD poster boy

to powerful spokesman for the Almighty? Great question. Two things happened in Moses's life and in mine. First of all, Moses found out he was not alone on what he thought was a God-forsaken mountain. As it turned out, God was the one who was actually there with him, just waiting for the right moment to let him in on the second thing—the secret.

The secret? What secret? The secret so crazy that it set bushes ablaze. God revealed to Moses that all of that junk in his life, all those deficits he thought were the reasons his life was pathetic and worthless—yeah, those were the exact things God was going to use to make his life one that both history and eternity would never forget.

AN UNLIKELY SPOKESMAN

Moses spoke with a speech impediment—a stutter, perhaps. We do not really know the reasons for his struggle with speech. He could have been born with it. Maybe his days as a youth in Pharaoh's palace were spent facing ridicule and disdain from his Egyptian peers.

"You're so stupid, Moses! You're not even a real Egyptian! Your own slave mother didn't even want you! What's the matter? Are you gonna cr-cr-cry?"

Of course, not all of what they were saying to him was true; but then again, what does truth have to do with anything when it comes to teenage cruelty?

Perhaps his speech deficits developed from some form of post-traumatic stress disorder after he murdered that Egyptian. Maybe he just could not shake the memories. When we read the Bible, it is easy to let the stories come off as sterile and unrealistic. When we read that Moses murdered someone, we immediately skip to the part where he fled into the desert. But think of it in *CSI* terms: *murder, blood*. Maybe they struggled. Maybe he strangled the unassuming Egyptian. Can you hear the disgusting sounds of gurgling and crackling throat cartilage as a calculated Moses violently strained to squeeze the very last breath from his victim's body? I bet Moses replayed that mental moment every day of his life. *What was I thinking? I never thought that I would be a mu-mu-murderer.*

Who knows the cause of the stutter? No matter what the cause, the effect was a man ineffective at verbal communication. Add to that forty years of contemplation on the backside of the desert, and you have a dude who had lost every hope of significance. Maybe he knew he was supposed to be a deliverer for his people; maybe he felt the sting of regret from his actions. His guilt and shame may have been unbearable. *No hope. No redemption. No future.*

Then a voice spoke up from the burning bush, and everything changed. God called to him from the flames and declared to him that crazy secret we mentioned earlier: he was going to take *all* of Moses's deficits and use them to make him God's personal spokesman. *What? Are you sure? But I thought that Aaron, Moses's brother, was the spokesman.* I will get to that in a moment.

Have you ever watched the news when a high-profile athlete or a politician gets into personal trouble and his agent or lawyer steps forward to speak for him? His words are as smooth as silk. *Denial. Misdirection. Masterful ploys of defense and avoidance.* Yes, it is nice to have a spokesman around.

Moses? He was about as smooth as sandpaper. He did not

sweep his wife off her feet by wooing her with his sweetly recited poetry. No. He beat up a bunch of shepherds who were messing with her at her family's well, and presto! Marriage. Moses had a thing for letting his fists, or sometimes his shepherd's staff, do the talking. Why? It was probably because his mouth was not up to the task. If you have ever seen the classic Hollywood production of *The Ten Commandments*, just know that the real Moses was no Charlton Heston, with his booming verbosity and deliberately bold banter. The real Moses struck first and talked—or stuttered, I should say—later.

What about Aaron? Was he not the spokesman? We cannot forget that having Aaron speak on Moses's behalf was not God's original idea. He only relented and sent Aaron for this purpose after Moses's excessive whininess. But as time progressed, Moses did indeed step into his calling as spokesman. If you read the Exodus story, you will notice that at first Scripture says Aaron spoke for Moses (Exod. 4:30), but moving forward, more and more it says Moses and Aaron spoke together. Even in the early plagues, Moses was speaking to Pharaoh on his own (8:9). By the last plague, Moses was doing most of the talking. And after Egypt, we never again see a scriptural record of Aaron speaking for Moses in public settings. Aaron became the high priest, and Moses became the spokesman, just as God originally intended.

In fact, no other figure in the Old Testament spoke more on God's behalf than Moses. Oh, but that was not where he started! Back on that burning-bush mountain on the first day of Moses's calling, he received the unexpected from God. He was given a mission to speak out first and let God do the striking. He was told to take the most embarrassing part of his whole existence and use it to speak for the one whose voice created the heavens.

"Come on, God! You don't need a spokesman! Just wave your magic wand and whisk the Israelites out of Egypt. Besides, if you are going to use someone's voice, don't pick me! I'll only embarrass you and make you look foolish, as my words have always done. Besides, my reputation precedes me there, and not in a good way. The Hebrews resent me because I was treated like royalty while they slaved away in mud holes, and the Egyptians resent me because I am a Hebrew who killed one of their own. Hello? I'm a stuttering reject, and you want me to speak for you?"

"Yes."

Here's the thing: God could have chosen one of a million other people to do this whole spokesman thing. What a great story it would have been to see one of the slaves rise up and speak boldly on his people's behalf. A pull-yourself-up-by-your-sandal-straps kind of guy with glistening muscles from his life of hard labor in the sun. A popular public figure among the Hebrews. Yet I wonder if being a slave still brought with it the potential for pride. For whatever reason, God did not choose them, or at least, if he did, they did not respond to his voice.

No, God chose a pretty boy—a stammering hothead who had been rejected by both sides, a man with a history of murder, a man with no voice.

THE CHOICE TO GO

God's direction. Moses's walking. God's power. Moses's staff. God's call. Moses's voice. That was the deal. The mission God had for Moses did not make things easy for him; it just made them clear. Make no mistake; Moses had a choice to face the mission, to speak out with a voice he hated, to walk publicly in the place of his greatest shame, or to stay quiet and hidden.

College was the mountain where my burning-bush moment occurred. I had to face my deficits. I had to face the "stutter" of my ADD, my lack of academic ability, and my seeming inability to make a difference. I walked among a campus full of brilliant scholars. Spokesmen of their generation. Scientists. Mathematicians. Authors. Future politicians. I took classes with them, shared the cafeteria with them, and lived in the same dorms with them. However, I dwelt in a stammering struggle far away from where most of them lived. Yet I knew God was calling me to be where I was. It was confusing. It was difficult. It was exactly what I needed.

So, like Moses, I made the choice to set out and face my issues and to let my life represent God despite my obvious inabilities to do so effectively. I found tutors in every subject. I found people who would proofread my papers for me. I faced the mostly well-meaning voices of reason—teachers and professors who literally told me, "Reggie, not everyone can do what you're trying to do. If you don't succeed, it's okay."

Another one said, "It takes a lot of people to make the world go round. Maybe you were meant to push a broom. There is nothing wrong with pushing a broom." The real kicker came when a professor told me, "You're not going

> I KNEW GOD WAS CALLING ME TO BE WHERE I WAS. IT WAS CONFUSING. IT WAS DIFFICULT. IT WAS EXACTLY WHAT I NEEDED.

to accomplish anything." I was the voiceless pinky toe of everyone's expectations just waiting to be pulverized.

Still, I walked forward just as the flaming bush had said. As I did, God created a moment for me that changed everything. The professor I had followed to NCBC, Rick Olsen, invited me to accompany him to a middle school assembly in Minneapolis. He asked me to share for five minutes about my life and my story. So I did. When I looked up, I began to realize that my words were either making or breaking those students' days. They were hanging on my every word, listening to my voice, yet hearing the one who had called me to speak.

That day I found my voice. I am not trying to say that I am like Moses. I am trying to say that we are *all* like Moses! We each have a long list of reasons our voices should not matter in this world. We each have a story to share. And guess what? Having a voice that the world already wants to hear does not necessarily mean that it is a voice God can use. Why? It is because our own abilities and accolades might deliberately or inadvertently do the striking. We might walk into Pharaoh's palace speaking silky-smooth words, yet have no power to back them up.

Moses might not have been the best speaker, but you better bet everybody listened. Staffs slithered around like snakes, locusts and frogs cascaded down so thick that you could not see the sky, and water turning to blood got everyone's attention. He spoke. God struck! That was the agreement, and it was a good deal.

It still is. That middle school moment suddenly brought life to the *death walk* of college academics I had been treading. I had a voice, and it was in the very place my history and shame were the greatest: schools. That very fact meant God could do in people the miraculous things I could never do, even with the slickest, most polished presentation. He wanted someone who was broken so people would focus not on the pretty glass vessel but rather on the refreshing liquid of life that was pouring out of it.

What's your story? What mountain taunts you with regret and shame? What deficit holds you in contempt of life and significance? Like me, like Moses, you have a choice.

Like me, like Moses, like the pinky toe, you also have a voice.

Oh, and that professor who told me I would never be able to accomplish what I was trying to do? Imagine his surprise when later on in life I was the keynote speaker at one of the university's graduations. He apologized profusely, but I had already forgiven him. I knew that my stutter was just the condition God needed to amplify my voice to the world.

Questions for Individual and Group Reflection

1. Reflecting upon the pinky-toe story, in what ways do the little things in life really matter?

   _____

   _____

2. Have you ever felt that your voice was too small to be heard? How does this make you feel?

   _____

   _____

3. Can one voice truly make a difference, or is that just a myth? Explain.

   _____

   _____

4. How did Reggie's academic struggles forge his character? What struggles are you facing that might be forging character in you?

   _____

   _____

5. What were the reasons Moses was an unlikely spokesman for God? How might the story have changed if Moses had been more qualified?

   _____

   _____

6. Why are our deficits not limitations to our potential?

_____

_____

7. In his first middle school assembly, Reggie discovered his voice. Have you ever had an experience when you first discovered your voice?

_____

_____

8. If you have not had such an experience, what choices can you make now to impact God's use of your voice tomorrow?

_____

_____

9. How did God's miraculous signs and wonders bring credibility to Moses's voice? What kinds of things will God do in our lives today to back us up when we are speaking on his behalf?

_____

_____

10. We know God does not need our voices, so why do you think he desires to use them anyway?

_____

_____

CHAPTER 7

THE "BORN" IDENTITY
KNOW YOUR NAME

ADVENTURES IN MOVIEGOING

So you have probably figured out by now that I am a sucker for a good action movie. Sylvester Stallone is my boy! *Rocky* . . . *Rambo* . . . it does not matter. My dream movie would be Rocky Balboa joining John Rambo with boxing gloves and machine guns blazing to free a full platoon of POWs from a Vietnamese prison camp—a camp where the head of the prison guards is a championship boxer who challenges Rocky to a twelve-round bout to the death!

Ooh, and what if Harrison Ford swooped down in the *Millennium Falcon*, landed in the jungle, and began swinging from tree to tree with his whip as the Indiana Jones we all grew up loving to cheer? And I am talking about the *real* Indiana Jones from the first three movies, who fought Nazis in search of historical artifacts, not the imposter from the last movie who fought Communists in search of a ridiculous alien skull. (Sorry, Spielberg, I just call 'em as I see 'em.)

Ah, there is something about a hero's name that sticks with you. Indiana Jones. Rocky Balboa. Luke Skywalker. Reggie Dabbs . . . okay, so surely I jest. The name is the reason little boys fight over who gets to be who when it is time to play.

"No, *I* want to be Iron Man!"

"You *always* get to be Iron Man!"

"I'm going home and telling my mama!"

For kids and for us, a name brings with it the character and characteristics of the hero who bears it.

Names work both ways, though. That is why there are certain names that repulse you when you hear them. Maybe it is an ex-girlfriend's or ex-boyfriend's name. Maybe it is a bully from your childhood who took your lunch money every day. The name itself is not bad; it is the memory or impression of the person you once knew who bore that name that makes your stomach churn when you hear it.

One of my favorite new heroes is a guy whose name is familiar to most moviegoers in the modern era: Jason Bourne. Most people consider Bourne to be the modern American version of James Bond. The funny thing about this hero, though, is that he starts out not knowing his name at all.

I love the opening scene of the first movie, *The Bourne Identity*. The camera shot is a hover over rippling waters in the middle of a vast ocean. No land in sight. No boats on the horizon. In the darkness your eyes are drawn to a faint, distant blinking light. A slow zoom reveals that the light is attached to a body floating lifeless in the deep. A man lost at sea is bobbing up and down like an unanimated buoy.

A small vessel fishes him out of the water. Surprised that he is alive, the benevolent captain cares for his wounds. When the mysterious man regains consciousness, we discover that he has absolutely no idea who he is. He has gunshot wounds. He obviously is in some sort of intelligence or in law enforcement, but he is totally devoid of any memories that would reveal his identity.

Thus, the adventure of discovery begins for our hero, and thus it begins for us.

THE NAME GAME

When Jason Bourne regains consciousness, the fact that he can speak does not mean he knows who he is. Finding our *voices* does not mean we automatically find our *names*. I know what you are thinking: *Reggie, I know my own name! I'm not an idiot!* But the kind of name I am talking about is not the designation you or I have been called by our families and friends since childhood; of course we know those names. I am talking about something deeper. I am talking about identity.

There is a gargantuan difference between our names and our identities. I knew that my name was Reggie Dabbs, but after that life-changing experience in my first public school assembly, I embarked upon the journey to identity. It was not just a search of what I was gifted to do; more important, it was about finding who I was supposed to be.

The journey to identity is a game that many play, but few ever win. Just imagine that your identity could be summed up in one word—one word that describes what you are all about. What would your name be? For many in this world, their one word would be *selfish. Bitter. Prideful. Drifter. Confused. Unteachable. Me.*

Man, that is a lot of pressure, isn't it? Finding one word to summarize your entire life's meaning. Up to that day in the middle school assembly, my one word was unknown to me but probably could have been chosen from a list of words: *Abandoned. Hapless.*

Deficient. Searching. Even though my name was Reggie and I had found hope in life, I did not yet know my identity. I had a voice, but I did not yet know how I would be known. But one thing was certain: the journey to finding my identity had taken a significant turn.

Most people look for their identities in what they do. Jobs. Interests. Talents. It seems so natural. Unfortunately, though, it is a dangerous thing to become identified only by what you are good at *doing*, instead of who you are good at *being*. Life consists of both doing and being, but one's true identity is defined by being. For example, just take a look at how many politicians in this world have accomplished significant things in their careers, only to ultimately be remembered for a moral or ethical failure. Even for athletes, the headlines are riddled with stories of how bad "being" choices eclipse one's amazing "doing" ability. As two talented freshmen from my favorite college football team found out in 2009, after robbing a campus convenience store with a pellet gun, one's entire future of *doing* can be changed in an instant by a lack of knowing one's identity. Full-ride scholarships and the potential for millions of dollars in future NFL earnings were all gone in a bad-choice instant.

> LIFE CONSISTS OF BOTH DOING AND BEING, BUT ONE'S TRUE IDENTITY IS DEFINED BY BEING.

Sure, what we do might arise from who we are, but there is a real danger in becoming competent at doing something before we have discovered and embraced our true identity. *Identity.* One word that sums us up. That one word that will forever describe who we are. That one word is called our name.

WHAT'S IN YOUR HAND?

If we return to the burning-bush moment on the mountain, we find that God asked Moses a funny question. The answer to which you do not have to be God to know. Anyone standing there would have known the correct answer.

"Hey, Moses! What's in your hand?"

I am sure Moses was already pretty freaked out by the magnitude of the moment. Leaves were flaming with red-hot fire, but they never burned up. God was speaking directly to him and calling him to do something beyond his ability. Then, this seemingly illogical question came. Moses probably looked down and figured that things were already so weird that he might as well go ahead and answer.

"Um, a staff?"

Before God sent Moses to use his voice against Pharaoh, God revealed to Moses a little bit of his identity. What was the significance of Moses's staff? It was a simple stick. Nothing spectacular. Moses had walked around with it for forty years. He had used its curved end to pull lost sheep out of danger. He had used it as a weapon against predators or even rustlers coming to steal the flock. Again, it was just a stick, but it was a stick he knew quite well.

It was as if God was saying to Moses, "Before you go do what I've called you to do, understand that even though you've been completely unaware of it, I've been forging an identity in you."

We always focus on the fact that Moses's staff turned into a snake when he threw it down. We remember the amazing aspects of the staff, such as when Moses raised it over the Red Sea just before it miraculously parted. We visualize Moses using it to strike a rock in the middle of the desert, producing a gushing river of water deep enough to quench the thirst of hundreds of thousands of thirsty Israelites.

Those were incredible *staff* moments, but the staff meant more to Moses's identity than just what unbelievable things he would do with it. It signified the process God had been accomplishing in him all those years in the desert. From prince to pauper. From riches to rags. From influence to obscurity. From confidence to insecurity. From statesman to stutterer.

Most important, it demonstrated Moses's morphing from royalty to shepherd. Ah yes, Moses's future would include some of the most staggering events in history, but God chose not to send him to go *do* until he had learned who to *be*. Don't just *do* deliverance, but rather *be* a shepherd.

What's in your hand? A staff. A simple stick that provides rescue and protection for sheep. Sheep. Stinky, stubborn animals that never say thank you and often wander off aimlessly into danger. Herd them. Corral them. Lead them toward water and away from cliffs. Know that they will always need you.

Back in Egypt, prior to "flee into the desert for forty years and become a shepherd," I think Moses probably already possessed the abilities necessary to do the job of delivering the Israelites. He may have even been more confident. Bolder. More influential. But God needed Moses to *be* more than he needed Moses to *do*. Therefore, God allowed the harsh desert climate to smooth the rough edges off of a once-flashy royal family member. All that was left was a shepherd.

"What's in your hand?" A staff. Not a scepter or a whip. Not a sword or a book. Nothing that we would expect to find in the grasp of a mighty deliverer.

"What's your name, Moses—your identity?" One-word answers came quickly. *Simple. Seasoned. Smooth. Steady. Subservient. Strong.*

One word. *Shepherd.* Guess what? Now that Moses knew who he *was*, God was ready to *do* more in Moses than he had ever imagined.

THROW DOWN YOUR SAXOPHONE

My voice was developing, but God was still forming my identity. In fact, he is still forming it today. But in those early days, God used the desert of college to shape me and to teach me my name. I fought hard. I found tutors. I decided that I would beat it.

In the midst of that process, I looked down to see what was in my hand. What I found there was not a football; it was a saxophone. The instrument that had brought me trouble, as a young kid who did not want to

practice, and ridicule, as a high school student stuck between two social worlds, now elevated me to places I never thought I would see. In reality I was a natural player. Music was inside my bones, and it did not take much for it to make its way out.

I also came to the wonderful conclusion that the honeys loved the saxophone. I never realized that in high school, so I never used it to its full potential. But soon I learned that college girls loved athletes *and* musicians, so I was set! I would be on a date, and I would reach for the sax to impress the lovely lady. I felt as if I had hit the jackpot.

Soon, though, news of my saxophone skills reached well beyond the college dating scene. Our school had a traveling gospel choir whose director invited me to audition for him. After a few moments of hearing me play the sax, he took me aside and told me that if I would play in the choir's band, he would make sure I got to see the world. That sounded great! I agreed, and a new adventure began.

The saxophone took me all over the United States and eventually all across Europe. The boy with no dad and no hope, who had never seen anything, somehow found his way to faraway places such as Norway, Sweden, and a host of other countries. When God asked me what was in my hand, I never dreamed he had plans to use that woodwind instrument to change the course of my life.

I still had to face the academic struggles of college, but my abilities with the sax gave me confidence and opportunities to perform in places I never could have reached on my own. The thing was, though, my newfound voice found room to speak in places to which my saxophone opened the door. I began to share my story with more and more people. Soon I was being asked to come play my saxophone and stay to tell my story. My name was beginning to morph, but the conduit of that change was not at all what I expected. Who knew that all of those music lessons when I was a kid—all those lessons I hated so much—would be the staff in my hand?

Just as Moses's identity as shepherd spoke volumes to those complaining sheep he herded through the desert for the next forty years, my identity as a musician was beginning to resonate with the very people to whom God had called me to take my message. I began to walk into schools and assemblies where a message of hope and love would most definitely fall on hardened hearts and deaf ears. Yet just a few smooth notes on the sax instantly changed the room.

Students who never had listened to any speaker in any format were suddenly hanging on my every note. Laughing. Singing. Swaying with their buddies.

When I finished a few songs and lay down the sax, I realized they were also hanging on my every word. Reggie the Saxophonist became one of my new names—an identity that brought greater credibility and effectiveness to Reggie the Public School Speaker.

CAPS, GOWNS, AND OPPORTUNITIES

I fought my way through the rigors of college, and eventually I found the finish line. I, Reggie Dabbs, earned my college degree! That process was the weight that strengthened the muscles of my resolve. I came to truly believe that dreams can become reality if you are willing to fight for them, and if you are willing to chase them down and make them happen. I walked across the stage. I wore the cap and gown. I left that commencement service with my college degree in hand, and no one would ever be able to take that piece of paper away from me. Graduation was the end of a major season in my life . . . and the beginning of a new one.

Fresh out of college, I continued full force into the whirlwind adventure of travel, playing the sax, and speaking. My musical talent began to place me in the company of some incredible individuals. I found myself playing in various bands and events with people like Whitney Houston and CeCe Winans. That was the season when I began to become more comfortable with being onstage in front of thousands and thousands of people. My nerves were learning the ropes of a lifestyle I had no idea was coming toward me on the horizon.

It was at an event with one of those artists that my life encountered the next huge avenue of change. The artist was someone better known in those days than he is today. He went by the name Carman, and he used to pack out stadiums all across the world. He produced fifteen gold and platinum albums and sold more than ten million records. He also holds the world record for the largest solo Christian concert in history. I was slated to play saxophone with him at the Tennessee District Assemblies of God Youth Convention in Nashville, Tennessee, on Thanksgiving night. It was a homecoming of sorts for me to be back in Tennessee with so many friends I had met while attending various camps and events during my childhood. Little did I know how huge that moment would be to the formation of my identity and my name.

The speaker who was booked to communicate to those two thousand or so students gathered at the magnificent Opryland Hotel was Dave Roever. Dave is one of the most easily recognizable people on planet Earth. This is not just because he is a phenomenal communicator, although he certainly is. You cannot really miss Dave because his face is completely disfigured.

Dave is a Vietnam veteran who was burned beyond recognition when a phosphorus grenade blew up in his hand. He had been in Vietnam for eight months serving as a riverboat gunner in the U.S. Navy's elite brown-water force. He was about to throw a grenade at the enemy when it exploded in his hand, leaving him severely wounded. He was hospitalized for fourteen months and underwent multiple surgeries. Against all odds he came out of the experience alive, but his body and face were completely deformed from the incident.

Over time and through his extreme physical suffering, he found faith in a relationship with God, and the state of his spiritual existence was as drastically altered as his face. He became one of the most sought-after speakers in the nation, taking his effective story and his masterful skills as a pianist into schools, arenas, stadiums, and veterans' hospitals.

I was excited about sharing a stage with him on that cold night in Tennessee. Little did I know, however, that his plane was running late due to extreme weather conditions and that a huge room full of students was staring at an empty stage. So the youth director who was in charge of the event came to me in desperation and asked if I would speak to the students for about twenty minutes, just to give Dave time to arrive. I wholeheartedly agreed.

I took the microphone and began to use the new voice within me to tell the story of pain and hope that had become pretty familiar to me by that point. It was a great moment in time; I was able to share the details of my past and how I had found love and forgiveness in my relationship with Jesus. I had no idea that Dave Roever had arrived just as I started my speech and had listened to the whole thing. After he was introduced, he immediately took the microphone and told the whole audience that I was his new assistant.

We had never even met, but I soon discovered that he had been asking God on that very night to help him find the ministry assistant he had been looking for. I was blown away! That day my life changed . . . again. I began a new part of my journey that would take me all over the world with an influential man who would personally influence me for life. He was a key component in the forging of my identity as a national speaker.

That frigid November evening, Dave Roever called my name, but I know that a much bigger voice was echoing through his. God himself was calling my name and revolutionizing my identity.

NAME RECOGNITION

There is something about saying someone's name. We have all experienced the awkwardness of forgetting the name of someone we run into periodically on campus or at the office. You should know it, but you just cannot snatch it off the tip of your tongue. At this point in the relationship, you cannot ask what the person's name is because that would be offensive.

In an episode of his famous sitcom, *Seinfeld*, Jerry Seinfeld experienced that exact scenario when he dated a girl for several weeks, but he never really knew her name. Their relationship was going really well, but the fact that he did not know her name was making the potential for disaster exponentially greater with each passing day. Jerry found ways to anonymously address her in the hope that eventually he would somehow stumble upon her identity. "Oh . . . you!"

When she discovered the truth, the relationship came to an abrupt halt. It was a hilarious episode, but if you have ever experienced a similar situation, then you know that the laughs are fewer in real life. Speaking someone's name is the basic form of personal communication. I cannot tell you how many millions of students I have spoken to over the years who simply wanted someone in their life to learn and use their names with affection, instead of apathy or abuse. So many sit alone at lunch. Sit alone in class. Walk alone through huge corridors, surrounded by a huge world of social interaction in which they feel like aliens, thinking, *If only someone knew my name or cared enough to learn it.*

Jesus knew (and knows) the value of names. He spent three years of his life on earth walking around with people whom he called by name to accompany him on his miraculous journey. Just imagine being one of the twelve disciples on the day Jesus called their names. What a crazy idea! The Creator of all things cared enough to know a fisherman's name and mention it.

Learning and calling a name is the launching point of any relationship. It is also the sustainable aspect of intimacy. When certain people we know begin to become close, we link their names together. "Oh, Jeffrey is coming to the party? Is Janice coming?" The mention of one name automatically generates an assumption or a question about the other name.

That happened with Jesus and those he called friends. People began to associate their names together. When they saw Jesus, they expected to see Peter, James, John, or a short list of others. Their names went together. Their identities were connected.

When this happens, we also become familiar with a voice that calls our names. If you were to place my wife in a room full of people, blindfold me, and have each person in the room call my name randomly, I would most definitely know the exact moment my wife speaks the word *Reggie*. Why? I have heard her call my name for many years now. Sometimes with tenderness. Sometimes in anger. Sometimes just to ask me to stop eating the food off of her plate. No matter the context in which she has said my name, the results are the same: familiarity, recognition, and intimacy.

The people who traveled with Jesus were not all men. The Bible is clear that Jesus had a host of female followers as well. He knew their names just as well as he knew the old Trusty Twelve. One of these female friends was a woman named Mary Magdalene. Before Mary met Jesus, her life was pretty messed up. Jesus changed all of that just as he has done for so many of us.

The day came when all those who personally knew Jesus faced the gravest of confusing circumstances. They believed and were certain Jesus was the Savior of the world because they had walked with him for three years and had witnessed things no human beings had ever beheld. Blind people seeing. The Deaf hearing. The disabled running. Even dead people living. For the friends of Jesus, the case was closed. What more could be done besides the amazing things Jesus had accomplished? He was most definitely God's Son sent to save the world.

Then one day out of nowhere, he died. He died? He died! Can you even begin to fathom the emotions his friends and followers must have felt? It was impossible that he could die. They had seen him bring dead people back to life, for Pete's sake! (Simon "Pete," that is.) Somehow the most unthinkable event they could possibly imagine became a brutal reality right before their eyes. The one with the greatest capacity for mercy in the universe was mercilessly beaten beyond human recognition and nailed to a wooden crossbeam in complete view of all of heaven and earth. No rescue from angelic warriors. No healing of himself with the same power he had used to heal so many others. No, he died seemingly as any ordinary man, by one of the most vicious and grueling processes of torture known to humanity.

Mary. Friend. Believer. Devoted. Dumbfounded. Devastated. Like the caption beneath a magazine photo of a family gathered outside the ruins of their beloved home that had been standing in the path of a class-three tornado the day before, the caption to this moment in Mary's life no doubt read, "What now?"

WHAT NOW?

Mourning is a state of mind. Intense emotion, sometimes coupled with anger or guilt, leaves those in mourning desperate for answers. Sometimes they take actions that are seemingly rash or illogical in a subconscious, despondent attempt to just do something . . . anything. Mary was no different. On the third morning she woke up from her continuing night terrors that resulted from the front-row seat of the destruction of her world as she knew it and decided to do something about her pain. She went to Jesus' tomb with the intention of mourning and caring for his body with special spices and oils.

Illogical. Why? Because she knew they had rolled a huge stone over the entrance to the tomb that she could never move. Out of her right mind with mourning, she went anyway, no doubt just to do *something* to ease her pain.

When she arrived, to her surprise the stone was already rolled to the side. She stooped to look inside the entrance, and her already seeping emotional wounds were suddenly ripped open with the realization that Jesus was *gone.* Someone had stolen his body. What more could happen? Mary was finished.

As she looked inside, though, she noticed two strange-looking men dressed in dazzling white getups as if they were on their way to some holy disco. They asked her why she was crying.

She freaked out: "Why? *Why?* Because someone has stolen the body of the Son of God!"

One of the men put out his hand to try and get her attention. "It's okay, he has not been stolen; he's alive!"

He might as well have been speaking Greek (or Hebrew in this case) because she apparently did not hear a word. Ignoring his incredible news, she ran out of the tomb and back into the garden. The reservoirs within her that she thought were completely drained of all tears suddenly found new depths, and she began to weep uncontrollably. Grief clouded everything, and there was no chance of an atmospheric break in the clouds.

And as if things could not have gotten even worse, one of the gardeners walked up beside her and interrupted her moment. All she wanted was some privacy—the nerve of some people! Obviously curious at the sight before him, he inquired, "Um, why are you crying?"

Mary looked up at the man and started in on him. "Look, they've taken away the body of Jesus . . . you know, Jesus? The Messiah! The one who healed thousands and was supposed to change the world . . . the one they murdered!"

The man seemed to be listening to her words, but he made no response. Mary became increasingly frustrated over his obvious ignorance of the events of the past few days. In desperation she finally just pleaded with him, "Look, if you took his body away or if you know where they have taken him, if you saw anything in the night when the robbers came, if you can do anything, please just help!"

What happened next changed everything. No long explanations were made. No verbose counseling techniques were used to comfort this severely distressed woman. No, just one word was spoken, and it did the trick.

"Mary."

I can only imagine the initial shock and confusion Mary must have felt when her name was spoken by this Stranger. Her head shot up, and her eyes lassoed him. She did not recognize him at first. He was average height. He had scars on his face, no doubt from a childhood accident. He was not much to look at. But then she saw his eyes, and the truth cascaded into her heart with double the force of Niagara Falls.

"Jesus? *Jesus!*"

NAME CHANGES EVERYTHING

Isn't it amazing that the angels had already told Mary the greatest news on earth before she ever heard it from Jesus? She was the first person to ever hear it! However, the mental state she was in somehow deafened her ears to what they were really saying. Grief or discouragement or insecurity or fear or a whole host of other things can do that to a person. When you are desperate, what you need can be spoken plainly but still have no effect. Sorrow can even make you miss two angels right in front of you.

It was not *what* Mary needed that changed things; it was *who* Mary needed that sealed the deal. Of all the multifaceted complexities of the historical, theological, and eternal significance of the moment, Jesus chose to begin the revelation of his resurrection with one simple word: *Mary.* Saying her name was the most intimate, loving, caring, and compassionate thing he could do. It was only four little letters (in our English translation), but it spoke volumes to her.

What is even more astounding is what his saying her name did to Mary's voice. She had already been given the news of his resurrection, but it was not until he called her by name that she ran with it and told the world. Mary was the first human to ever proclaim the eternal message of the ages, yet she almost missed it entirely. When Jesus said Mary's name, though, her identity changed from "hopeless mourner" to "bold messenger." That name meant that Jesus still knew who she was, that he still cared about her, and that he had not given up on her, even though all seemed to be lost.

As I continued my own journey and hit the road with Dave

Roever, I knew God had called my name. He had redefined my identity. I had intellectually known what he did to save the world and me, but when he began calling my name, I felt empowered to become his personal megaphone. He knew me. I knew him.

The name Reggie had once meant "bastard kid." He called me *Prince*. Once I was *Misfit*; he called me *Champion*. My value was once twenty dollars; he called me *Priceless*.

Mary had to show up at the tomb to throw down what she had. In her case, spices, oils, and tears. I had to show up and throw down what I had as well. Insecurity. Deficiency. Saxophone. Speaking. All of it, good and bad.

> WHEN JESUS SAID MARY'S NAME, THOUGH, HER IDENTITY CHANGED FROM "HOPELESS MOURNER" TO "BOLD MESSENGER."

What do you have to throw down? Those things are not meant to define your identity. When God calls your name, because you know him and he knows you, your new identity will begin to emerge—a *reborn* identity.

Questions for Individual and Group Reflection

1. What is your favorite adventure movie? Name the hero in that movie. What mental images does this name generate?

   _____

   _____

2. What are the differences between a name and an identity?

   _____

   _____

3. Can you think of one word that describes your identity up to this point in your life?

   _____

   _____

4. What are the dangers of becoming competent at what you *do* before discovering and embracing who you *are*?

   _____

   _____

5. What was the significance of the staff in Moses's hand? Why do you think God told him to "throw it down"?

   _____

   _____

6. How does the name *Shepherd* describe the mission that God had for Moses? What other one-word names could Moses have been called?

_____

_____

7. What are your reflections concerning the role of the saxophone in Reggie's identity development as a nationally known speaker?

_____

_____

8. What things "in your hand" seem to be unlikely instruments that God could use in your life? How could you throw them down?

_____

_____

9. What is the difference between hearing a stranger say your name and hearing someone you know very well say your name?

_____

_____

10. Like Mary, the truth will only make sense in our lives when we hear the intimate voice of Jesus calling our names. Have you ever heard God call your name? If not, take a moment to ask God to make himself known to you.

_____

_____

CHAPTER 8

FROZEN PLANES AND FAKE EARS

KNOW YOUR PASSION

SURF'S UP ... STAIRS

When I was a kid, I loved to swim. What kid doesn't? We did not grow up rich or anything, so it was not as if we had our own swimming pool. If I wanted to swim, I had to go to one of the public pools or the YMCA. Unfortunately, though, I did not get to go very often. *Bummer.*

But one day I decided I would not let my passion for swimming be repressed simply because our

family owned no pool. It was time for a little Reggie creativity. It was time to take ownership of my situation and make something out of nothing. I put on my swimming trunks and scoured the house until I found where my mom had stowed all of our beach supplies. I grabbed a couple of my favorite floats, and then I waited. Patiently. Deliberately. Diabolically.

Finally the moment of opportunity presented itself. My parents left the house for a few minutes to run an errand. My time had arrived, and I seized the day . . . as well as the bathtub faucet, turning it to full blast. I had thought this out in detail. I stuffed a few towels under the door and sat back, waiting for my swimming pool to materialize.

It came through with flying colors . . . or swimming colors, in this case. Soon I was wading with floats and rubber duckies in my own personal indoor swimming pool. Very indoor. The depth of water came to two or three feet, but my excitement was immeasurable.

As I splished and splashed amid the floating bathroom debris, I heard a car door close outside. My heart dropped. I don't know what it is about being a kid that causes your reasoning skills to be completely suspended. It is as if you are living in some alternate reality where whatever you do right now in the present has absolutely no bearing on what happens to you in the future. In "Kiddom" you can eat an entire bag of Halloween candy with no possibility of puking your guts out later. You can place a thin ring of superglue on the seat of your teacher's chair and not go to detention. You can even scale the roof of the garage and execute a dive that would make Spider-Man jealous and not have to take a trip to the emergency room.

In this case you can even create a makeshift swimming pool in the upstairs bathroom of your house without being caught and punished for it, or so I thought. Shoot, maybe I would even be praised for my ingenuity and creativity. Yeah, that alternate kid reality came to a screeching halt.

I was not downstairs to see it, but my guess is that Dad figured out that something was wrong the moment he stepped across the threshold of the front door. That was probably due to the bulging drywall of the ceiling and the multiple streams of water cascading down into little pools all over the floor. I could hear his massive steps climbing our staircase, and for a split second I contemplated trying to fit myself down the drain of the tub. Hey, I figured I could have quite the life of adventure and intrigue living alone in the sewer system like some pre–Ninja Turtle with an Afro. No, I could not fit, so I was forced to just wait for the inevitable.

Dad reached for the doorknob, turned it, and then immersed himself in a tidal wave that included a young boy bodysurfing his way toward the stairs in a desperate attempt to escape the certain death that awaited him. In true Go-Go-Gadget fashion, Dad reached out and detained me in an instant with just one of his colossal arms. The other hand he kept free for another purpose that I will not disclose here, but you can rest assured that I did not sit down on any poolside lawn chairs—or any chair, for that matter—for a long time.

My family most definitely questioned my wisdom that day. They questioned my sanity. They even questioned my desire to live. But do you know what they did not have to question? My passion for swimming. My actions that day forever solidified for me and those around me that I loved water, and I loved swimming.

Passion, you see, emerges somewhere in the intersection of desire and action. We are usually most passionate about something we have tasted just a bit. I never knew how much I loved ice cream until my mom gave me a little bite. After that, I was passionate, and I have spent the rest of my life pursuing this frozen treasure in any form on most every continent of the globe. I even threw back a cone in Antarctica. Hey, you don't have to worry about it melting!

To find and become acquainted with your true passion,

> *IT WAS TIME TO DO MORE THAN JUST WADE AROUND IN THE CALL I FELT ON MY LIFE; IT WAS TIME TO GET SOAKING WET AND MAKE SOME WAVES.*

you must have a desire and a taste. For me, I had been given a voice and a name that meant something different than when I started out in life. I knew I was set apart to speak to people, especially students, on any scale available. From my first go at it, I was even pretty effective. My story did the trick every time. I had a genuine desire, and I had tasted the tip of the sweet iceberg, but little did I know that the next stage of my life would ignite a passion in me that would set the course of my steps for years to come. It was time to do more than just wade around in the call I felt on my life; it was time to get soaking wet and make some waves.

It was time to know my passion. It's your time too.

THE ULTIMATE WRESTLER

The story of Jacob is one of intrigue, adventure, and deceit. When you really break it down, Jacob was quite the little shyster. He was always looking out for *numero uno*, making sure he got exactly what was coming to him.

It all began at the homestead of Jacob's father and mother, Isaac and Rebekah. Jacob was the youngest of twins. Rebekah had had trouble conceiving, and Isaac asked God to grant them children. God answered, and Rebekah became pregnant. However, something weird began to happen: Rebekah felt what the Bible calls "a struggle" within her belly. Now, I do not know exactly what it feels like to be pregnant, but I am sure the last thing a mommy wants to feel is something struggling in there. So Rebekah asked God why this was and if everything was okay. God answered by telling her that she was pregnant with twins and that two separate nations would result from them. He also told her that the older son would serve the younger son.

In those days that was a huge deal because the older son was always the favored one. He would receive the largest inheritance and carry on the family name. To say that the younger would be stronger and more influential than the older was to say that the younger son was bound to be a bit different.

Boy, that was an understatement! The struggle Rebekah felt inside her womb was just that: a prebirth wrestling match between the two brothers. Talk about sibling rivalry. These guys were duking it out before they even made their respective journeys through the birth canal. Now that is hard-core!

That was Jacob's nature; he was a wrestler from the beginning. When the two boys were finally born, the first son came out, and the Bible says he was "like a hairy garment all over" (Gen. 25:25). Nice. I did not start seriously shaving until I was almost twenty years old, and this dude was covered with his own bearskin rug straight out of the womb. They called him Esau, which meant "hairy." Not *Harry* but *hairy*. Now, that's a social limiter.

You might think that people laughed at Esau, but you would be mistaken. Esau, you see, was a man's man in every sense of the term. Hairy, scary, and quite contrary. He was also a hunter extraordinaire. He would bench-press boulders and strike matches on his face. He was just the son every man dreamed of in those days, and his daddy, Isaac, loved him with all his heart. Isaac loved him mostly because Esau would go hunting and bring back Isaac's favorite game, possibly venison, prepared just the way he liked it. Ah, now, that's my boy!

Jacob, on the other hand, was not defined by his hairiness. Quite the contrary, he was identified by the fact that he had a death grip on his brother's heel when he emerged from the womb. That little tiger had wrestled with his big brother for nine months and was not letting go, even on their birthday. He did not want to come out second; he was determined to be in first place from the beginning. So they called him Jacob, which means "grabber" or "deceiver."

Jacob was the antithesis of his twin, Esau. While Esau was out with his dad hunting in the woods, Jacob preferred life back at home with his mother. He enjoyed the culinary arts. The Bible calls him a "mild man" (v. 27), which is another way of saying that he was a pretty boy.

Mama loved Jacob more. Daddy loved Esau more. *Ding, ding!* Let the fight begin. If the two had been professional wrestlers as we think of them today, Esau would have been the Mania from Mesopotamia while Jacob might have been called the Younger Brother Who Acts Like His Mother. Jacob could move like a butterfly and cook like Aunt Bee! It was the Homebody against the Body Builder.

To make a long story just a bit longer, Jacob never stopped *grabbing* for what was not his. He demanded to be first in everything. One day he waited until his brother was coming in from a long hunting trip and was famished with hunger. He whipped up a pot of sweet-smelling red-bean stew and wafted the aroma in his brother's direction, taunting him with the tantalizing smell. Overcome with seeming starvation, Esau foolishly agreed to trade his birthright—all of the things he would gain as the firstborn son—for a bowl of soup. Apparently, Esau's muscles had robbed his brain of some much-needed oxygen.

That should let you know just how shrewd and sneaky Jacob was. He connived and negotiated his way to an upper hand with every breath of his body. He was a sleazy salesman who could talk his own brother into the worst deal imaginable.

In Genesis 27 the plot thickened when their father lay on his deathbed and called for Esau to come to him so he could bless Esau with all of the inheritance that was coming to him as the firstborn. Esau went hunting one last time to kill and prepare his dad's old favorite: deer meat surprise. Meanwhile, back in the kitchen, Jacob and his mother devised a scheme. Jacob covered his neck and arms with sheep's wool and tried to disguise his voice to trick his old, blind father into giving him the blessing instead of Esau. Sidebar: how stinkin' hairy are you if someone can pass off as you with a big hunk of sheep's wool? *Whoa!*

Anyway, it worked, and Jacob received the blessing. King Kong (aka Esau) returned from his hunt with his deer meat surprise. And surprise! His blessing was gone! Hairy Scary Esau was spittin' mad and went on a rampage. He was literally going to kill his little deceitful brother. This time Jacob knew better than to stay and wrestle. He turned tail and ran to save his own skin—much smoother skin that appreciated just the right amount of moisturizer.

WRESTLING WITH PASSION

Jacob ran, but the Grabber was not finished grabbing. He ended up working for his uncle, a rich man name Laban, who had two daughters, Rachel and Leah. Jacob had a "thing" for Rachel and wanted to marry her. Laban agreed, on one condition: Jacob would work for him for seven years. Dude, now, that is the kind of dating requirement I wish we had today. "Sure, you can take my daughter to the movie, if you mow my lawn each week for seven years first."

Jacob loved that girl so much that he agreed to the terms and did his time. But lo and behold, Laban tricked him, and due to some very odd circumstances, Jacob ended up married to the other sister, Leah, instead. Jerry Springer would be in heaven with this story! Laban then convinced Jacob that he could also marry Rachel, if he would work *another seven years*. By this point, Jacob was fed up with Laban. You never con a con man.

Jacob agreed to Laban's plan, but he devised a plan of his own to make sure he got ahead on the deal by convincing Laban to let him keep all the sheep that had a certain spottiness to them. When the seven years were up, Jacob's few little spotted sheep had multiplied by the thousands, and he was a filthy rich man. Keep in mind that they did not have checkbooks or bank accounts in those days. Livestock was like gold—stinky gold that walked around and pooped on your lawn.

So the wrestler did it again. He faced adversity and found a way to work things out to his own advantage. He was a man of passion—passion for himself. He always found a way to make sure that, at the end of the day, he would be the one laughing last and laughing the loudest.

But judgment day finally caught up with Jacob. He found out that, after almost fifteen years, his brother Esau was ready to meet with him and exact the revenge he had no doubt fanta-sized about for years. I can only imagine how many times Esau had drawn Jacob's face on the side of a deer and sent it running across the field for a little target practice. This was the day of reckoning, the day Pretty Boy would have to own up to his lying ways and face the terror of Follicled Freak!

Jacob was terrified, so he did what he always did: he tried to weasel his way out of the situation. He took his wives and children and sent them ahead to meet Esau with an array of gifts and treasures. What a sissy! Who would send his own family ahead of him to meet his greatest enemy? For Jacob it was a pitiful effort at creating a smoke screen that he hoped would soften the heart of his hair-laden brother.

Then Jacob crossed over the river and stayed by himself the night before the big fight. For the first time in his life, he had nothing left to grab. His family. His money. His dignity. They were all on the other side of the river. He could not deceive or connive his way out of this one. He was finally face-to-face with the fact that the only thing he had ever been passionate about in life was himself, and that was not good enough anymore.

That is when it happened: the strangest wrestling match in all of history. The Bible records that some dude wrestled with Jacob all night long. We discover that the guy Jacob was fighting was actually God himself! Now here is the deal about wrestling with God: if there is even a fight at all, it is only because he is letting you live. God's headlock would end the universe as we know it. But God was not letting Jacob off the hook this time. It was time for him to face his selfish passion once and for all. It was time to come clean with his true identity.

After the wrestling match came to a God-allowed draw, God struck Jacob in the hip. Why the hip? I think it was because God was ready for Jacob to understand the nature of his own life and to discover where his passion should lie. The little guy who could always run fast enough to elude the consequences of his own actions would now walk the rest of his life with a noticeable limp. Every time he would slowly meander his way across the yard, he would be reminded that he had been a wrestler who had met his match on the other side of the river.

Then God did something else that changed Jacob's identity, literally. He gave him a new name: Israel, meaning "Prince with God." Wow! That's some upgrade! From deceiver to prince. God had called Jacob to be the next one in his family line to carry the promise of faith. He was the heir of the promise that someday a Savior who would change the course of the world and eternity would be born into his family.

But Jacob had always been all about Jacob. He had been passionate about things that did not matter. God was ready for Jacob to become passionate about . . . well, God. The promise and the calling that surrounded his life were to be his new passions. His new name and his new walk were reminders that the deceiver would deceive no more. From here on, it was time to face the music and let God lead him everywhere his leg would limp.

Oh, by the way, when he met Esau the next day, there was no fight. As it turned out, Esau had had a change of heart, too, and was ready to reunite with his brother in a way they never had before. The wrestling match that had started in the womb was forever finished. Both of them had lost, and both of them had won.

Mama's boy? Yeah, Jacob was no longer a weaselly little grabber of a pathetic man; he was now a prince of God with a new passion for living . . . and a limp.

FROZEN PLANES, BURNING HEARTS

I found my passion during the time I spent on the road with Dave Roever, and like Jacob, I would never walk the same again.

Dave was a sought-after speaker at citywide crusades, churches, statewide men's events, youth conventions, business conventions, military installations, and multiple other venues across the United States and internationally.

However, Dave's forte was most definitely the public school assembly. Besides the fact that he was an excellent communicator, he had a certain *wow* factor because of his extreme injuries. Kids do not necessarily like listening to speakers in assemblies, but even with all the teenage tactics of apathy, avoidance, and agitation they possessed, they could not ignore Dave's disfigured appearance.

The crazy part, though, was that as mesmerized as they were with him, he was even more enthralled with them and their situations. He had a passion for their condition and used the most painful and life-altering features of his history to relate to them. His scars were obvious. They were highly visible, even appalling. But Dave's words exposed the scars that were on the hearts of the students who listened to him. Hidden pain. Abuse. Selfishness. Hopelessness. His speaking events were the unlikely meetings of two different kinds of burn victims. One had experienced the literal pain of being seared by a grenade while the other had experienced the blisters of internal injuries inflicted from a hostile life environment. Both had experienced pain. Both needed healing.

Roever would travel anywhere anytime to find and speak truth to these kids. His pain taught him that everyone hurts even if their wounds are not visible on their physical bodies. He was passionate, and I was at his side. I knew how to speak in schools, but I did not know how to have passion in schools. My time with Dave taught me things I never could have learned on my own, taking me to a whole new level of passion for the students themselves, not just the idea of speaking to students.

Dave also taught me a lot about Vietnam. The fact that you

might think it odd that I would reference Vietnam in a book like this is exactly the reason I am doing it. I learned that Dave Roever is just one of thousands of Vietnam veterans who sacrificed life and limb for a war that his country called him to fight, but for which the people of his country did not necessarily understand or approve. Those young boys came home physically and mentally wounded, only to be met by many citizens of their nation whose backs were turned on them. In most cases they were neither appreciated nor thanked for their valor. Instead, they were met with corrosive disdain amidst a national atmosphere of political distrust and social upheaval. They were sometimes called *baby killers* and were literally spat upon by crowds of protestors who disapproved of the government's war policy in Vietnam. The media and press of the day were riddled with negativity over the entire issue. It may or may not have been a war that everyone understood or approved, but those young boys who spilled their blood in the jungles of Asia are nothing less than heroes.

My years traveling with Dave revealed to me his passion to minister to those veterans. They were still carrying the burden of a nation that never acknowledged their sacrifice. He used to say that it takes twenty-two miles to turn a huge navy battleship around in the ocean; it took twenty-two years for someone to say thank you to our Vietnam heroes. If you are one of those heroes or if you are a member of the family of one, consider this a personal message of thanks from Reggie. Your sacrifice is appreciated and is not forgotten.

Dave was about passion—passion for students, passion for vets, passion for people. His passion and his voice propelled him into a life of constant travel for the various bookings and events. He traveled so much that, eventually, he purchased his own private jet. When I boarded that plane with him for the first time, I thought I was really living high on the hog! Little ol' Reggie on a private jet. Who would have thunk it?

I will never forget one trip in particular that forever taught me the value of knowing one's passion. Dave and I were in Seattle at an event. We left the event late and headed to the airport to fly to the next destination. When we got to the airstrip, bad weather had set into the area, and the wings of the airplane had iced over. We were determined to leave, though, so we took matters into our own hands by getting buckets of hot water and pouring them over the wings. Yeah, sounds like a pretty exotic lifestyle, right? A big black guy and an old Vietnam vet on an airstrip, late at night, dousing airplane parts with buckets of water in the middle of a winter storm. We were a sight. We still are, I suppose.

The weather and the plane apparently did not intend to cooperate with our efforts that night. No sooner than we poured the water over the wings, it would freeze again. No, we were not going anywhere on that particular night, no matter how much we wanted to.

By this point it was crazy late. We found ourselves sitting down for a little healthy snack at Denny's about 2:30 a.m. Now, I do not mean to generalize, but there are some colorful people at Denny's at 2:30 a.m. I imagine they were thinking the same thing about us. After polishing off our grease-laden feast, we found our way to a cheap motel near the restaurant. It was about 3:45 a.m., and the ice storm was now angry and beating with frigid fury upon the roof and windows of the hotel lobby. There was no one at the front desk, obviously.

Dave reached out and rang the little service bell. No one came. He rang it again. Still nothing. A few minutes of ringing left us still standing there with nowhere to sleep and little chance of making it anywhere else in the maddening storm. Dave said, "Well, looks like no one's getting up for us tonight."

Just then from the darkness of the back room behind the desk a voice said, "I'll get up with you anytime, Dave Roever." An older woman emerged from the blackness. As it turned out, she recognized Dave because she had been watching him speak earlier that very night on a prerecorded television program. The story got even better. She was dealing with a great amount of doubt and insecurity concerning her relationship with God—another wounded soldier looking for healing.

As she had listened to Dave speak on television, she prayed, "God, if you still love me, send me a sign that you have a plan and hope for my life." Two hours later the very man who had been speaking to her through the airwaves stood at her little desk.

> GOD LET AN ICE STORM COME TO SEATTLE, WASHINGTON, SO THAT ONE LITTLE OLD LADY IN A NASTY OLD MOTEL COULD HEAR A PERSONAL MESSAGE THAT SHE WAS STILL LOVED.

She checked us in and gave us our room key. I headed on up to the room and collapsed into an exhausted heap. When I woke up the next morning, Dave was not in the room with me. I went down into the lobby to find him sitting at the same lobby table where I had left him. He was still wearing the same clothes. In front of him were a box of donuts and the hotel clerk. They both had tears streaming down their faces from the healing that had taken place during their all-night conversation.

That was just one of the moments when the realization of what passion is really all about set into my heart. God let an ice storm come to Seattle, Washington, so that one little old lady in a nasty old motel could hear a personal message that she was still loved. That she had value. That her life was worth living.

To find your voice is one thing; to learn your true identity is quite another. But to discover your God-dreamed passion is the very stuff of life. I knew I had been given the ability to speak and play my saxophone, and I had learned my identity. I even began to gain a name among people all around the world, but it took some time on the road with a man of passion to ignite real passion within me. I began to see the value of people in a way I never had before. God was not just calling me to be funny or to share stories about my life that made people cry. He was calling me to be passionate for what he is passionate about: people. To see the broken. The poor. The lonely. The hopeless. The unattractive. The rejected. The criminal.

My life began to be consumed with his fire, and I learned the ropes of what it meant to live this demanding lifestyle so that one person on the far side of the planet—in the backwoods of Appalachia, in the frozen cities of Russia, in the outback of Australia, in the busy streets of London—could hear the news that someone loves him. *That God loves him. That I love him.* Both loves became my passion.

I burned with the desire to change kids' lives. I wanted to use my voice, to be confident in my identity. My life is a pure adventure! It is not always an easy adventure, but it is always an eventful one. I usually wake up in some random part of the globe, speak at four or five schools during the day, and at night speak at a rally sponsored by a local alliance or ministry. My day ends with some sort of offer for the listeners to respond to the same call I responded to so many years ago. I issue a call to find a new identity, a call to embrace change and produce change in the world.

My passion stems from this: Somewhere in the world, a kid is going to bed on a Sunday night. She is hurting. Lonely. Maybe contemplating suicide. Maybe hiding the scars of self-inflicted wounds on her arms and legs. Maybe addicted to drugs. Maybe trapped in a sexual relationship. Just think, in one day, at one program, the direction of her life can be altered forever. When she lays her head on her pillow on Monday night, her life has been eternally changed because of just one day. The value of that one kid has become my passion, and that is why I am willing to travel from the frozen fields of the rural American Midwest all the way to the crowded villages of war-torn Africa.

Like Jacob, my time on the other side of the river was a season of wrestling. My whole life I struggled through the details to survive. I became successful, but I still had to face my heart. When you begin to face the motives of your pursuits, especially when your life has already been met with some

> *WHEN PURPOSE IS MET WITH PASSION, YOU NEVER WALK THE SAME AGAIN.*

level of success, that is when you discover the purpose planned for you all along. And when purpose is met with passion, you never walk the same again.

THE ULTIMATE MEMENTO

I like to think that each season or experience of life leaves us with a little souvenir, something by which to remember the moment. The day I fashioned the makeshift swimming pool on the second floor of my house, I took away the spanking of my life. For Jacob, his memento was not something he could hold in his hand but rather something he could feel in his hip. His reminder was made clear by the limp in his stride—a token of remembrance from God that his passion had changed.

When my time with Dave Roever was coming to an end, I decided to take a memento away from the experience. Dave is a very funny man, and one of his favorite things to do is to play the piano by ear. When I say *by ear*, I mean that Dave's ear is prosthetic, and he can take it on or off of his head. To play by ear for Dave means to take his ear off and hold it in his hand while playing the piano. It's a crowd favorite.

On the last morning we were on the road together, we were staying in the same room, and while Dave was in the shower, I noticed that he had multiple ears lying on the dresser. So I took one and stowed it away as a souvenir. I never gave it back, and up to now, he has no idea that I took it.

Sorry, Dave! Just know that I took away from our time so much more than just your ear; I took with me your passion.

Questions for Individual and Group Reflection

1. What are your reflections on Reggie's homemade swimming pool story? Do you have any similar childhood stories?

   _____

   _____

2. Is it easy to see passion in children? Why is that?

   _____

   _____

3. What aspects of Jacob's character made him a *wrestler* in every sense of the word?

   _____

   _____

4. What are the characteristics of someone who always looks out for number one? How does a person like that make you feel? Have you ever been that person?

   _____

   _____

5. Can you think of Bible examples when God called someone to be passionate about things other than him- or herself? Are there any examples where God did call someone to be passionate about self?

   _____

   _____

6. Have you ever "wrestled" with God? How does this kind of experience change the way you walk?

_____

_____

7. What are your impressions of the Dave Roever story? How did Dave use his own tragic circumstances to be passionate about others?

_____

_____

8. Considering the treatment of many veterans after Vietnam, what other choices could Dave have made about his passion? How might his story and Reggie's story have changed?

_____

_____

9. Do you have any "mementos" in life that remind you of your passion?

_____

_____

10. What passions do you feel God burning into your life? What choices can you make to turn these passions into actual life pursuits?

_____

_____

CHAPTER 9

GOMER'S ODYSSEY
KNOW YOUR FUTURE

MORE WITH THE AIRPLANE STORIES

I have probably spent as much time on airplanes in the past ten years as I have in cars. I am always flying. For that matter, some airline workers know me by name, not that I don't stand out just a bit.

I will never forget one flight in particular that demonstrated to me in full human HD and surround sound the concept that each of us is on a collision course with our futures (no pun intended). I was flying out of Detroit. We were waiting at the terminal to board the plane when I looked out the airport windows only to discover that the weather had morphed into a black vortex of destruction. The small trees planted around the airport were bent to horizontal. As it turned out, the entire area was under a tornado warning. *Great*, I thought. *I won't be flying anywhere for a while.*

As I was walking to one of the courtesy phones to book a hotel room for the night, I heard a female voice on the intercom system say, "Flight 245 with continuing service to Dallas is now boarding rows one through nine."

Wait a second, I thought. *That's my flight.* I approached the flight attendant at the gate and inquired about the safety of flying in these weather conditions.

"Sir, if it wasn't completely and totally safe, we would not be boarding." She seemed so confident, almost a little smug.

"Oh, okay," I replied, "then I guess you're going with us, right?"

She paused. "Actually, sir, no, I am not." That was not a very comforting piece of information. But it really did not matter that much. I am so used to flying that a little storm was not that big of a deal to me.

So we walked through the Jetway and boarded the plane. When I sat down in my seat, I glanced out the window at the guys who were loading our luggage beneath the plane. I noticed that one guy was basically holding the side of the plane and was laid out horizontal in midair like a character in some Looney Tunes cartoon. Not the best omen.

As I buckled up and prepared myself for what lay ahead, I heard something unexpected—someone was praying quite loudly across the aisle from me. It was a middle-aged woman, and she was getting with it! She was crying out for Jesus with every short breath that came from her mouth. I was ready for an altar call. I heard her say, "Jesus, don't let me die. Please don't let me die!"

Inwardly I chuckled. Outwardly I held it together. "Hey, are you okay?" I was sincerely worried about her.

"No," she cracked, "this is my first flight ever."

"Oh, man!" I exclaimed. "Well, listen, I fly like every week of my life, so I'll walk you through everything. All of this stuff, yeah, this is totally normal."

She seemed somewhat relieved, yet still obviously apprehensive. Just then another passenger came and sat down in the row in front of hers. Now, I am not the fashion police or anything, but he had to be the best-dressed brother to ever get on a plane. Just his shoes probably cost more than my entire wardrobe. It was obvious he was someone important, some influential titan of industry, or perhaps a broker on Wall Street. He did not seem nervous at all about the weather; in fact, he seemed a bit irritated because it was slowing down the boarding process. I could tell that, like me, he was no stranger to flying. He buckled in, took out his *Wall Street Journal*, and began reading nonchalantly, probably checking on how many millions of dollars his investments had garnered that day.

Hyperventilating Suzy, however, still mumbled desperate prayers under her short breaths. I figured I would help ease her mind a bit. "Look, I'll help you out. If I give you a thumbs-up, then everything's just fine and dandy. If I give you a thumbs-down . . . well, that's not so good." She seemed genuinely thankful for my offer.

Thumbs-up.

The plane taxied to the end of the tarmac, and the captain came on the intercom to give us an update. "Uh, evening, folks. This is your captain speaking, and it would appear that the tower has cleared us for takeoff."

Thumbs-up.

My anxious friend smiled back and let out a sigh of relief. The captain continued, "Yeah, to be honest, we're the only ones taking off tonight."

Thumbs neutral.

Captain Sunshine was not quite finished yet. "Yep, folks, I'd say that you're in for the greatest roller-coaster ride of your life. I'd definitely make sure that you stay seated and stay buckled because it's going to be pretty wild."

Thumbs-down.

I wish I could exaggerate what the flight was like, but it would be impossible. We shifted and zoomed our way between gusts of wind like some huge, metal teleporter. To call it a roller-coaster ride would be an understatement of epic proportions; it was more like skydiving in tandem with 150 other people. All the while I felt great. The lady across the aisle was holding on to sanity by a miniscule emotional thread, but she was still with us. The man in front of her just kept reading his paper as if nothing was out of the ordinary.

What happened next has an actual aeronautical description. It is called a "downdraft," and it occurs when the wind blows down instead of from left to right. At fifteen thousand feet, a sudden downdraft shot us straight downward about five thousand feet in three seconds flat. If you have ever ridden one of those zero-gravity drop-zone rides at theme parks, you can begin to grasp the sensation of what it was like.

The oxygen masks even dropped from the ceiling! I would have put mine on and "breathed normally" as those ridiculous instructions say to, but I was too busy laughing. The lady beside me had suddenly turned into a professional opera singer and had been holding a perfect high F note for about fifteen seconds: "Jesuuuuuuuus!"

And as if that were not enough, when we had somewhat leveled off from the downdraft, Mr. Moneybags threw his newspaper to the side, unbuckled his seat belt, and assumed a kneeling position right in the middle of the aisle of the plane. He whimpered at the top of his lungs, "Jesus, please forgive me . . . I'll do anything . . . don't let me die!"

We did not crash, and to this day, I haven't stopped laughing.

What that particular airborne escapade reinforced to me was how important the future was to each person on that plane. It is amazing how people act and react when they suddenly believe that the future is real . . . and that it is closer than they think.

LOVE AT FIRST SIGHT, COURAGE AT TWO YEARS

The future is an equalizer. It worries stay-at-home moms, and it worries CEOs of multimillion-dollar companies. It makes nocturnal worrywarts out of professional athletes as well as couch potatoes. When the weather of life is nice, we often do not think about it much. We just board the plane of living, put on our headphones, and wait for the free pretzels. But when the wind blows us sideways and downdrafts propel us toward the certain destruction of our happiness, our security, our health, or even our actual lives, that is when we start singing—or in some cases, screaming—the real melody of our future.

Up to a certain moment in my life, I had spent most of my time dwelling on the unchangeable circumstances of my past and the seemingly insurmountable deficits of my present. But eventually my future took center stage. You may think I have already told you a lot about my future. My success at public speaking. My opportunities to travel and to play music. The fact that I discovered my passion and calling in life. Indeed, we have journeyed through stories concerning these topics, but as we near the end of our journey together, I want to take some time to focus on a complete picture of what the future holds.

It is my hope that you discover firsthand all the things we have talked about up to now. I pray you learn to know your past, even the parts that are stuck in perpetual Tuesdays. I hope you find your voice and discover your real name by discovering your identity and throwing down what you have in your hand. All of these things play into your future, but there are other components necessary for fully understanding it. These components are less about what you learn or what you know and more about who you know and how you learn to love and serve them.

For me to return to the point in my life when my future really took shape, I would take my mental time machine to a little church in Detroit. As you just read, later in life I would encounter a real tornado in Detroit; but early on my heart was met with a hurricane in the same city—a love hurricane.

One of my college roommates was a guy named Mike Simpson. Mike became a youth pastor in Detroit after graduation, and he brought in a band I happened to be playing with for an event. It was there that the winds of my future began to swirl. While we were setting up and preparing for a sound check, a group of young women was helping to put out some new songbooks in the sanctuary of the church. As I looked up from my perch on the stage, my eyes beheld a vision of beauty.

She was the most gorgeous female I had ever seen. My knees became Jell-O, and hey, "There's always room for Jell-O!" I wish I could tell you I had the courage to walk up and ask her out that day. I wish I could tell you I had the courage to call her the next day and chat about life. Yeah, I wish I could say those things, but the truth is that it took two years for me to actually muster up the courage to talk to her like a human being.

When I did find the strength within me to communicate my true feelings, I simply asked her for this: one chance. I asked for one chance to try to be the man she would want and would need at her side in this life, one chance to prove to her that our future together would be better than our future apart.

You are probably thinking, *Dude, Reggie! A fine-looking brotha like yourself, why did you take so long to make things happen with your honey?* That is an excellent observation about my good looks, as well as an excellent question. I am glad you made them both. Here it is: I had embraced the gifts that had been given to me and had accepted the fact that my life was already miles ahead of what the world would have expected of a twenty-dollar misfit. I had a college degree. I had a steady job. I even had somewhat of a name for being a speaker and musician. I was not cocky about all these things; I was simply aware of them, and I had gained confidence that there were certain things I could do well.

But when it comes to your future, your real future, it is hard to shake your past. I'm talking about the stuff that you just know is preprogrammed into the intricate software of your mind. I had a great set of foster parents, but I just knew that someday my future would be suddenly altered by some genetic or hereditary tendency or mental state from one or both of my biological parents—some unknown, hidden pollutant floating about in the gene pool of my psychological makeup that would one day spontaneously produce horrible things in me. In other words, I was always worried that I was incapable of being a decent husband, much less a good one. Concerning this most crucial part of my future, there was nothing natural within me from which to pull. All I had in my bloodstream was bad blood.

I always wondered if I was going to someday end up like my real father. Absent. Addicted. Apathetic. I know it may seem like an irrational fear to you, and in many ways, it even seemed irrational to me. I had a great childhood and a family who loved me and taught me how to be the right kind of man. In the end, though, my future concerning marriage or fatherhood was always viewed through a hazy lens of my own history—a history for which I was not responsible. Still, I was shackled to it.

GOMER'S ODYSSEY

One of the most peculiar accounts in all of Scripture tells an unlikely story about God's viewpoint on our pasts and futures. It is the story of the prophet Hosea. My interpretation of the story may be a bit different than any you have heard before, including the one found in the book of Hosea. The facts are all there, but I've always been astounded at what drama the people in this story must have experienced.

Hosea was a God-follower in every sense of the word. A holy man. A man of devotion and faithfulness to God in every way possible. I also think he was probably a younger man, due to the fact that he was unmarried. Just imagine a young, single minister whose heart is pure and who wants to fill his life with only the things that please God. Dude, Hosea had it going on!

One night after he had finished his studies in the Scriptures, he got down on his knees and prayed, "Oh, God, thank you again for this glorious day. I know you are everything that matters to me in life. Tonight, once again, I just ask that, if you ever see fit to bring a wife into my path, you would prepare my heart to know how to love her just the way you love me. Thank you, God." He got up, brushed his teeth, blew out the flame in his lamp, and lay down to sleep.

At 1:30 a.m. he was awakened from a dead slumber by the

actual, audible voice of God. He was stricken with wonder! How many people in the world ever get to hear God's voice? He felt so alive, so free! God said, "Rise, my servant. Go and find your bride."

Hosea's heart beat faster than a caffeine-riddled rabbit playing a drum kit! He dressed himself as quickly as possible, while still maintaining a neat look, and headed out to the street to find the love of his life. His hair was spiked just right, and he even wore his lucky blue jeans. This was it—the moment for which he had been saving himself all these years.

He walked down the street and he heard God say, "Turn left." He turned. He walked. God said, "Turn right." He turned. He walked. He stopped dead in his tracks, and God said, "There she is."

Before him, leaning against a lamppost, was a picture of beauty beyond his wildest dreams. His heart leapt within him as he approached her. She winked at him and said, "Going my way, sailor?"

Hosea giggled like a schoolgirl. "I'm not a sailor, but I bet your father was a thief, though, because he stole the stars from the sky and put them in your eyes."

She laughed but not wholeheartedly. Something told him that she was no stranger to cheesy pickup lines. "You're cute," she said. "What's your name?"

Name. Name? Come on, dude, pull it together! Hosea was so love struck that it took him thirty seconds to remember his own name. *Harold? Hezekiah? Hank? Liechtenstein*? "Hosea!" he finally sputtered. "I'm Hosea."

She ran her fingers through his hair, sending a shiver down his spine. "Hosea, eh? I like that name. I'm Gomer."

Gomer? Present-day sidebar: If your name is Gomer, and you are female, in our culture you would be thrown to the proverbial wolves of ridicule. Your lunch money would be permanently distributed via direct deposit into the account of Bullies Anonymous. Simply put, you would be a social outcast. But Hosea was so mesmerized that he did not even bat an eye.

"Gomer," he mumbled clumsily in a siren trance. "That's the most beautiful name I've ever heard."

There is one thing you should know about the lovely Gomer, something that, if you have not already figured it out, will color your viewpoint of this story. There was a reason Gomer was leaning against a lamppost at 1:53 a.m. She may have looked like a model, but she was no model citizen. She was a bad girl if you know what I mean. She was not the kind of girl you take home to meet mama. Have you figured it out yet? I will just spell it out: Gomer was a prostitute.

Let it all sink in. Hosea was a guy as pure as the driven snow, who was awakened by God Almighty and told to go out to meet his bride. Whom does he meet? A prostitute. Now, how would you like for that to be your story? You wait your whole life for God to reveal your one true love only to be led down the street to a corner where men came to solicit women for sex. I'd think you would be confused; I know I would.

Hosea, however, embraced God's plan for his life and fell head over heels in love with Gomer. She could not believe it. He was the first man to ever open the door for her. He was the first man to compliment her, instead of crudely shouting inappropriate innuendos in her direction. He was the first man to say she was beautiful and mean it for the right reasons. He was the first man who did not attempt to sleep with her. Oh yeah, she had it bad for him too. She fell for him, and for the very first time in her life, she had the right reasons to fall.

They were married; it was a short engagement. His friends and family were supportive, but he could tell they were talking about him behind his back. A "girl like that" cannot be good for someone's reputation, especially a minister's. He never wavered in his love for her. Her friends? She did not really have any. Hosea was the first person she had ever met who really loved her.

The honeymoon was filled with passion and delight. Their romance was deep and meaningful, everything for which they both had dreamed. Months of marriage turned into years, and though Hosea never faltered in his feelings for Gomer, something within her was beginning to flail. She could not quite place it. Here she was, finally loved, finally safe, yet the lifestyle of her past began to resurface in her dreams. The danger. The intrigue. The lack of commitment. The lack of pressure to be somebody she wasn't. Her guilt over her past soon morphed into guilt over missing that past. What was wrong with her? She just did not know.

Married life became mundane and predictable. Hosea was the same loving man he had always been, but Gomer could feel herself drifting. After two years of marriage, she became pregnant. She gave birth to their first son and named him Jezreel, a name that literally meant "revenge." She had another child, a daughter named Lo-ruhamah. Her name meant "not loved." Then another boy came along named Lo-ammi, which meant "not my people." Just the names of their children alone should have been a warning sign to Hosea of trouble to come.

Hosea was ecstatic to see his children born, yet he knew that something was wrong with Gomer. She was somehow slipping away from him, and he felt powerless to stop it, despite all the love he continued to show her to keep her close. Then the night came. Hosea came home from work to the sounds of two babies screaming. Jezreel, the older boy, was about six years old and was sitting on the floor just inside the door. He was mumbling to himself, seemingly oblivious to the spectacle of the other children.

Hosea swept in and made everything right. He changed diapers, fed the children, and put them to bed. He did it all because Gomer was gone, maybe forever. That night he sat at her dresser with his eyes closed. He took a bottle of her perfume into his shaky hands. He had saved for a year to buy it for her on their first anniversary. It was the most expensive thing he had ever purchased.

He pulled out the cork and let the sweet aromatic scents of his bride rise into his nasal passages and take him away to a time many years before when they were both intoxicated with each other's love. Now, he was the only one still addicted. He pulled out a piece of paper and began to write: "'She decked herself with her earrings and jewelry, and went after her lovers; but Me she forgot,' says the LORD" (Hos. 2:13). He dotted all the *i*'s with the watermark of his own tears.

Eventually he fell into the trance of sleep, but it was not really rest. His mind was tormented with worry and shame. He knew exactly where she was, and even if he went and convinced her to come home, he was not sure he could ever bring back her heart. About 3:30 a.m. he felt the sheets move as she quietly climbed back into bed after her nocturnal activities. He saved the blowout for the next morning; he did not have the energy that night, and he feared he would do something crazy.

The next morning did not disappoint. They went back and forth for three hours. They both screamed. They both cried. They both arrived at a place of no resolution. From that point on, the scenario repeated itself often. She would disappear, sometimes for days on end. He would tend to the children each night and painfully transcribe the sonnet of his soul: *She decks herself with rings and jewelry and goes to meet her lover. But me? She forgets.*

THE LOVE AUCTION

One night when she was gone, Hosea heard Jezreel mumbling to himself again. This time, though, he picked up on some of the words. *But me? She forgot?* Hosea scooped him up, and they both cried. Gomer's unfaithfulness was killing his family; yet against all odds, he still loved her. He still saw her value. He hated her life, but he loved his bride.

Then it happened. The day he had hoped for against all hope. She showed up at 9:00 p.m. Her nose was bloody and her clothes were torn. She had been beaten up badly. She again knew, as she once had known, what this life was doing to her and her family. She fell on the floor and took hold of Hosea's ankles, begging him for forgiveness and promising to change.

Hosea did not hesitate. He picked her up in his arms and carried her straight to the bathroom. He gently sponged the blood from her face. He tended to her wounds. He cleaned her up and put her to bed to sleep it off. All was well. The children did not cry. The family was back together.

For a few weeks everything was pristine. It could not last, though, because her heart was sick, seemingly beyond recovery.

She disappeared again one night. This time, she did not come back. Three days passed. Then three months. Then a year. It was over. Hosea mourned, and most nights he could still be found penning his least favorite words amid the alluring smells of a bride he once held in his arms. He pulled it together during the day, but his heart was halved, and he knew it. Somehow the memories of his bride and her absence made his heart grow even fonder of the love they once had shared but was now gone forever. He was tormented, only because he still loved her.

One day he was walking through the local marketplace, shopping for groceries for the kids. They had not missed a beat as far as the necessities were concerned. He had done everything, but it did not replace their mother. God had not spoken to him in a long time. But now, out of nowhere, the unmistakable Voice rang out again in his ears: "It's Thursday. It's auction day. Look at the auction."

Hosea was not so keen on replying to him immediately this time. He knew what kind of auction was held on Thursday. It was not the selling of livestock; it was the selling of slaves, specifically, female slaves.

"I can't do it, God! I won't buy a slave anyway. And besides, those women are naked! I don't need to look."

"Yes, you do. Look at the women on the auction block."

God's command was strange, but Hosea felt he had no choice but to obey. He turned aside and let his eyes gaze upon the host of nude women who stood before him. He blushed at first, just trying to be technically obedient without being lewd or sleazy. He decided the best strategy was to focus on their eyes. He was the only man in the entire crowd—a crowd shouting bids and waving money—who was actually looking at their eyes.

Then he caught them. Those eyes were familiar. About ten women back his eyes locked with Gomer's. She looked like a skeleton. Her eyes were bloodshot, and her hair was matted. She looked as if she had not eaten a decent meal in days. When she saw him, tears began streaming down her face. They were tears of regret and shame. It seemed that she had finally hit the bottom; she now understood the extent of her decision and the value of what she had thrown away in exchange for a temporary mirage of adventure.

Now she belonged to another. Hosea would never want her back anyway. What kind of husband would take back a woman like that?

Hosea, that's who! As always, he did not hesitate. He sprinted away from that auction block, knowing he did not have much time before she would be fodder to the highest bidder. He flung open the door of the house and began fiercely rummaging through every nook and cranny for any scrap of money he could find. The kids were curiously drawn to his bizarre actions. He told them their mommy was being sold at the auction. A short silence ensued before a unanimous decision was reached: "Let's buy her back, Daddy!"

Now their little hands joined his in the ransacking. Coins. Bills. Heirlooms. Anything they could find was thrown into a pile on the living room floor. As he ran his hand wildly under the bed, his nose caught a familiar scent. It was her perfume flask, the top still removed from his writing session the night before. He grabbed the flask and examined it. It was still over three-fourths full; it was worth more money than anything else in the house.

He grabbed the children and headed out into the street. He was hesitant to take them to such a dangerous place, but he was fully cognizant that they would follow him anyway. They were quite the sight—a desperate family running recklessly down the street, arms full of trinkets and baubles, the lingering scent of a costly perfume wafting in the faces of those they zipped past.

THE COST OF YOUR FUTURE

I leave you at this point of the story because it is the moment that might just define your future. I know what you are probably thinking: *Gomer did not deserve Hosea. What guarantee does he have that she won't go back to her old life again? How could Hosea let his children go through that?*

God called Hosea to marry a prostitute. Then he called him to buy her back with all he had. God's ultimate purpose? To show Hosea and all of Israel how *he* felt about *them*. God had been a faithful husband to his people though they had repeatedly given their hearts to another. Though they were destitute and undeserving of redemption, he still saw their value. He still wanted to buy them back.

He still does! He finds us when we are trash, when we have no hope, when our futures are secure in the bonds of meaninglessness. He woos us with his love and invites us to know him. To live life with him.

Oh, but we are so prone to wander back, inexplicably drawn to the mirage of our old lives. We repent; then we sell ourselves again to a world that beats us up and drains us of all value. We reason that God is angry with us, and surely he is. But his anger is not the sort that demands revenge. Rather it is an anger based on not only what could have been but also what still can be. It is a passion to regain the relationship. He writes the poetry of his love for us in the skies, in his words, in his mercy, in the very midst of our adultery.

I could not know my future because I felt the sentence of Gomer over my own personal life. I was definitely Gomer in the story, not Hosea. I was the one whose past seemingly sealed my future. I was destined to be horrible at being the right kind of spouse and parent, but God demonstrated through Hosea's experience that he was willing to spend all he had to purchase us from our past. In fact, that is exactly what he did when he poured out the priceless treasure of Jesus. Jesus cracked open his own life and let the sweet aroma fill the earth. Priceless, yet free. God ran to my auction and bought me back. He also paid to buy *you* back!

I know, I know. Gomer had no business being redeemed. So true. However, the extreme story of Hosea and Gomer shows us exactly the extent of God's willingness to take us down from the stark nakedness of our shameful situation and love us again. He has chosen to make us a part of his future. But what was supposed to keep Gomer from doing it again?

Nothing but Hosea's love and her choice.

She might have gone back, but she did not have to. I could have ended up as a horrible father and a deadbeat husband, but I learned that the price Jesus paid to set me free from the slave auction of my past also created the potential for me to choose my future with him. I was free to choose to be a faithful husband. I was free to choose to be the kind of biological father I never knew myself. I was free to build my future by building my marriage and my family.

I asked Michelle for one chance. Nineteen years later she

is still giving me that chance. Our marriage is not perfect, but thankfully we have never experienced the anguish that Hosea and Gomer faced. Our marriage is a reflection of the choice we both have to embrace the future God has so expensively purchased on our behalf. The extravagance of God's perfect love has opened the door for love to be unconquerable in our home. No matter how bad the day is, no matter what issues we may face, we can be confident that the Hosea-love of God has already been lavished upon us. Therefore, we are free to lavish it upon each other.

Marriage was a milestone of my future, but it was not the ending point. It was the beginning of another adventure. For you, maybe it's time to let God set you on the adventurous course of your future. His choice has produced choices for you. You do not have to be the alcoholic. You do not have to be the one shackled by pornography. You do not have to be the fearful one or the angry one. What a price he paid!

> THE EXTRAVAGANCE OF GOD'S PERFECT LOVE HAS OPENED THE DOOR FOR LOVE TO BE UNCONQUERABLE IN OUR HOME.

It was no doubt an emotional moment when Gomer saw her family running toward her to buy her back with their greatest treasures. At that point the only thing that could hold her back from redemption was her own guilt, regret, and fear. If she wanted it, though, a future was waiting for her with open arms.

Fair? Who said anything about fair? This is grace, and grace really isn't fair. But it is free. Free and fragrant!

Questions for Individual and Group Reflection

1. What are your reflections on Reggie's downdraft story? When people are in danger, what can we see about them?

   _____

   _____

2. How is the future an "equalizer" of people from all walks of life and all social statuses?

   _____

   _____

3. Do you think Reggie had legitimate concerns in his two-year hesitation in approaching Michelle? Why or why not?

   _____

   _____

4. Have you ever read the story of Hosea in the Bible? How did Reggie's version of the story change your perceptions of it?

   _____

   _____

5. Do you think God was fair in commanding Hosea to marry Gomer? Why or why not?

   _____

   _____

6. If you were Hosea, would you have taken Gomer back? Why or why not?

_____

_____

7. Would the story of Hosea be the kind of love story people would want to hear today? Why would it differ from most modern love stories?

_____

_____

8. Though we know the cost Jesus paid for our future, how does the story of Hosea and Gomer reveal the heart of God toward us?

_____

_____

9. Does God's willingness to take us back mean that he never gets upset or angry with us? If God is willing to buy us back, what occasions would arise in our own lives that would warrant us not forgiving those who have wronged us?

_____

_____

10. What issues of your future do you need to address with a new perspective? What choices do you now have as a result of the love and high price Jesus paid for your freedom?

_____

_____

CHAPTER 10

BIG DADDY
KNOW YOUR FATHER

NURSERY DRAMA

Well, here we are—our final chapter together. Most chapters of this journey together have begun with some funny or crazy anecdote from yours truly. However, I would like to cap off our excursion with a story of a different kind that might not be as amusing but is definitely as important.

Michelle and I were married and were living our new life together the best we could. A few years in, she became pregnant. I was excited. I was terrified. By this point, I knew that I was not sentenced to be the biological father I never knew. I understood that my family and my future were both parts of my choice. But I suppose that any prospective dad is terrified.

There is so much to consider when a new baby is entering your home. What will he look like? Will he be born healthy, or will he have special needs? Will he look like his mama or me? (I prayed about this one.) Shy or outgoing? Talkative or quiet? Studious or artsy or both? No matter what I felt I was or was not prepared for, our baby was on his way. Game on!

We prepared the best ways an expectant couple can. Baby furniture. Paint. Diapers. Car seat. Blankets. However, there is only so much for which new parents can prepare. What I could not predict was the drama of the day our son was to be born.

Michelle went into labor about midnight. I rushed her to the hospital, which is a story unto itself. We were living in Dallas at the time, and when we left the house, we ran into a construction detour. So I took a shortcut. Michelle looked at me and asked, "Um, are you sure this way is quicker?"

Hmmm, let's see. She's in labor, and I am supposed to be the man of the hour. Sad to say, I lied. "Sure, I'm sure!"

Well, that shortcut turned out not to be so short. I somehow managed to find the only brick road in all the Dallas–Fort Worth area. My wife was none too thrilled with the miles of bumpiness that ensued. My shortcut was almost a dead end to my marriage. Somehow, though, I managed to get us to the hospital. But as it turned out, there was no need to hurry. She would be in labor for twenty-eight hours. It was too long, and I had a bad feeling.

With a concerned look on his face, the doctor called me out into the hall. I was terrified. "Reggie," he said in the sober tone that only a physician can produce, "I'm afraid that if Michelle and your baby are both going to survive, I'm going to have to give her a scar. We need to perform a C-section immediately, or I don't think they're going to make it."

In moments like those you have little choice but to agree to whatever is necessary. My heart was in my throat. On that surgical table lay nearly everyone who was important to me in the entire world. I had dreaded for so much of my life the commitment and pressure of being the kind of husband and father I had never known; but now, I was pleading with God for the chance to try.

The C-section was performed, and my prayers were answered.

Michelle came through with flying colors, and my son—my boy, Dominic—finally made his appearance in the outside world. The man whose life had been defined by the actions of a bad biological father was now a father himself. My dad was not there when I was born, but I would not have missed my boy's first cry for all the money in the world. My future became ever so much clearer on that magical day in the hospital.

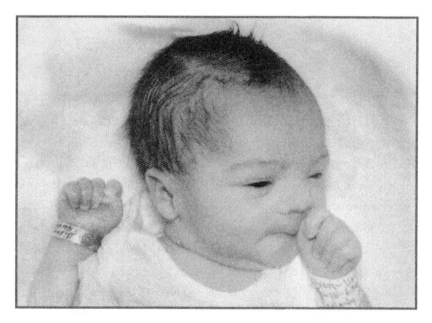

From the get-go I found myself doing things and feeling emotions that had never before surfaced in my life. I immediately began counting fingers and toes. Ten of each. That's my boy! As Michelle went into recovery, the nurses whisked Dominic away to the newborn nursery for observation. Michelle had tried to convince me to go home and take a nap while everybody else rested. I agreed, but instead, I secretly made my way to the hospital nursery and camped out near my son.

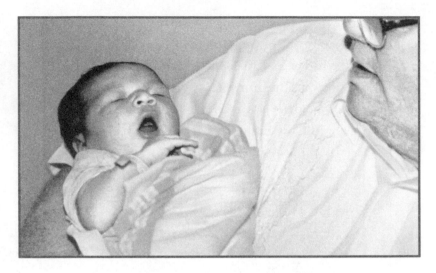

Gazing at him through the window—his little eyes not yet able to see me, his little ears not yet familiar with or attentive to the sound of my voice, his little body not yet comfortable in my arms—I was there, and I would not leave. I watched his chest move up and down as he took swift and innocent little baby breaths. I cringed as the nurses ruthlessly but necessarily pricked his heel and tested his reflexes. He had no idea that I was there or even who I was. Oh, but I was there, and I was now his little life's protector. He was my baby; I was his father. I was his big daddy.

FATHER FIGURES

Fatherhood is a touchy subject these days, and it should be. For just a moment consider with me some alarming statistics about the role of fathers in our nation. According to a 2009 U.S. Census Bureau report, more than twenty-four million children live apart from their biological fathers. That breaks down to one out of every three (33 percent). For African Americans, nearly two out of every three children (64 percent) live in father-absent homes. One out of every three Hispanic children (34 percent) and one in four white children (25 percent) do not have a dad at home.[1]

Okay, but is a child's life truly affected by the lack of a dad at home? The statistics may shock you. Consider just how it affects a child's socioeconomic status. Children in father-absent homes are five times more likely to be poor.[2] A child with a nonresident father is 54 percent more likely to be poorer than his or her father.[3]

But an absent father does not hit children just in the wallet; it also makes a huge difference in their health and well-being. Based on birth and death data for 217,798 children born in Georgia in 1989 and 1990, infants without a father's name on their birth certificates (17.9 percent of the total) were 2.3 times more likely to die in the first year of life.[4] One study revealed that single mothers were twice as likely as married mothers to experience a bout of depression. Single mothers also reported higher levels of stress, fewer contacts with family and friends, less involvement with church or social groups, and less overall social support.[5]

Take it for what it's worth, but researchers also found that toddlers living in stepfamilies and single-parent families were more likely to suffer a burn, have a bad fall, or be scarred from an accident, compared to kids living with both of their bio- logical parents.[6] Psychologically, a study of 3,400 middle school children indicated that not living with both of their biological parents quadrupled their risk of having an affective disorder such as depression, ADHD, or bipolar disorder.[7] These types of disorders contribute to other physical health problems as well. Children who live apart from their fathers are more likely to be diagnosed with asthma and experience an asthma-related emergency, even after taking into account demographic and socioeconomic conditions.[8]

If that is not enough, just consider how not having a dad living at home affects behavioral development during childhood and even into adult life. Even after controlling for income, youths in father-absent households still had significantly higher odds of incarceration than those in mother-father families. Youths who never had a father in the household experienced the highest odds.[9] In a 2002 Department of Justice survey of seven thousand inmates, it was revealed that 39 percent grew up in mother-only households. Approximately 46 percent of those inmates had a previously incarcerated family member, and one-fifth of them experienced a father in prison or jail.[10]

A study of 13,986 women in prison showed that more than half grew up without their fathers.[11] Even controlling for community context, there is a significantly higher percentage of drug use among children who do not live with their mothers and fathers.[12] Youths without a highly involved father are more at risk of first substance use. Living in an intact family also decreases the risk of first substance use.[13] In one study involving 228 students, those from single-parent families reported higher rates of drinking and smoking, as well as higher scores on delinquency and aggression tests when compared to students from two-parent households.[14]

The numbers are staggering when the issue of teen pregnancy is related to present and active fathers in the home. Being raised by a single mother raises the risk of teen pregnancy, marrying with less than a high school diploma, and forming a marriage where both partners have less than a high school diploma.[15] Separation or frequent changes in family dynamics increases a woman's risk of early menstruation, sexual activity, and pregnancy.[16]

A woman whose parents separated between her birth and her sixth birthday experienced twice the risk of early menstruation, more than four times the risk of early sexual intercourse, and two and a half times higher risk of early pregnancy when compared to women in families that were still together. The longer a woman lived with both parents, the lower her risk of early reproductive development. A woman who experienced three or more changes in her family environment exhibited similar risks but was five times more likely to have an early pregnancy.[17] One study out of the U.S. and New Zealand found strong evidence that father absence has an effect on early sexual activity and teenage pregnancy. Teens without fathers were twice as likely to be involved in early sexual activity and seven times more likely to get pregnant as an adolescent.[18]

Then there are issues of abuse for those who do not have both parents at home. Compared to living with both parents, living in a single-parent home doubles the risk that a child will suffer physical, emotional, or educational neglect.[19] These kids have a 77 percent greater risk of being physically abused, an 87 percent greater risk of being harmed by physical neglect, a 165 percent greater risk of experiencing notable physical neglect, a 74 percent greater risk of suffering from emotional neglect, and an 80 percent greater risk of suffering serious injury as a result of abuse.[20]

The issues of education are affected greatly by the presence of fathers or the lack thereof. Fatherless children are

twice as likely to drop out of school.[21] Father involvement in
schools is associated with the higher likelihood of a student
getting mostly As. This was true for fathers in biological parent
families, for stepfathers, and for fathers heading single-parent
families. Students living in father-absent homes are twice as
likely to repeat a grade in school; only 10 percent of children
living with both parents have ever repeated a grade, compared
to 20 percent of children in stepfather families and 18 percent
in mother-only families.[22]

A 1997 study found that in two-parent families, children
under the age of thirteen spent an average of 1.77 hours a day
engaged in activities with their fathers and 2.35 hours doing
so with their mothers. Children in single-parent families spent
only 0.42 hours a day with their fathers and 1.26 hours with their
mothers.[23] Half of all children with highly involved fathers in
two-parent families reported getting mostly As through twelfth
grade, compared to 35.2 percent of children of nonresident
father families.[24] A study of 1,330 children from the Panel Study
of Income Dynamics (PSID) showed homes that have a father
who is involved on a personal level with his child's schooling
increases the likelihood of the child's achievement.[25] When
fathers assume a positive role in their children's education, students feel a positive impact.

THE FATHER-FACTOR

Okay, surely I have made my point. Fatherhood is an issue
that is shaping the future of our children in more ways than
most people realize. If you think back to those names I gave

to students in the first chapter—names like Champion, World Changer, and History Maker—maybe you are beginning to realize why I began this book by telling you about my mission to be a daddy to millions of students all across the world who either do not have one or do not understand what one is supposed to look like.

You cannot just tell people they have choices and need to change; there are legitimate reasons most of us struggle. There are foundations underneath the faulty structures of our emotional, relational, and spiritual houses, and these foundations have cracks. Our concept of father—and *the* Father—is often the starting point as these cracks begin to spiderweb out, like a wounded windshield.

It is hard to pick just one story from the Bible to illustrate how God feels about the father-factor; in essence, it is the theme of the entire book. Skeptics may disagree with this statement, but the context of the biblical narrative as a whole is replete with the concept. Prove it? All right, I will.

Let's start from the beginning: Genesis. When God decided to create the earth, he did so in grand fashion, like a Tony Award–winning Broadway production that comes to town and sells out the playhouse seven nights straight. He flicked the sun into its burning existence, like hitting a simple light switch. Like a confident and deliberate cosmic conductor, he dramatically orchestrated elaborate, melody-rich movements of tides and land and leaves and fish and birds in perfect sequence, the metronome of his own grandiose wisdom keeping it all in perfect time. Animals burst forth from the deserts and jungles and plains, all varieties and a multiplicity of beasty species. It was just another mammoth multitask of the Creator, executed effortlessly at the cue of a few simple words. Child's play.

Child's play—that's it! When day six rolled around, God decided to make something different from the rest of the creation he had been fashioning. Now, don't get caught up in the imagery and miss the magnitude of what happened here. When God made man and woman, he deliberately formed them to be different from everything else he had created. Different from the trees. Different from the stars. Different from the snake.

They were the only aspect of creation that was not completely original. No, there was a blueprint for their design. It was God himself. He made them in his own image. Unlike the dog, God does not walk on four legs. Unlike the elephant, he does not have a trunk. No, God's features are similar to . . . well, ours. Don't think it sacrilege to indicate that God might look like us in some way; that was his point! He has hands; we have hands. He walks upright; so do we. What God did when he created humankind was to reproduce a likeness of himself in creatures of lesser understanding. Lesser power. Lesser glory. Lesser ability to grasp the full picture. What God did was produce *children*.

Our concept of children grows out of this concept in ways I doubt we fully realize. When we have a child, a less-powerful version of ourselves emerges from us. "Look, he has your nose. He has my eyes." Various traits are easily recognizable, but it is obvious that the little newborn lying helplessly in the hospital nursery is not the same as the parent from whom he came. Children are different, but they share a comparable image.

I can hear you from beyond the pages. "Easy there, Reggie! You're making the Bible into some hippie handbook where God is Daddy and life is a sandbox where he is watching me play with my friends." I agree that many have taken the father-factor and twisted it into a mockery of its original intention. They've made God the kind of father that our culture knows best, the one from the statistics we just read. This kind of father-God is absent most of the time, except on special holidays such as Christmas and Easter. He is usually too busy for us. Who can blame him? His work is very important!

He is buddy-buddy with us only out of guilt or simply because it is easier to leave harsh truths to the other parents of our lives. His time with us is short, so we had better make it fun. He always shows up with gifts for his little tykes, unspoken payment for not being there when we really needed him. We hope that he remembers to call on days that are important to us, and if he doesn't, we are mad for a while, but we find a way to make peace with the fact that he is just that kind of father. At least we do not have a father like some other friends of ours, one who is constantly asking them where they are going or making them do chores. Yeah, this father is easier to manage.

I hate to break it to you, but God is not a manageable father. He wants to know where we are. He wants to talk with us every day, just as he did with Adam and Eve in the coolness of Eden's late afternoon. He gives us tasks to do and is not afraid of looking uncool in front of our friends by disciplining us when we need it. He is definitely *not* manageable.

He is not even reasonable. As the author of reason, his viewpoint automatically qualifies as the correct one even when it befuddles the minds of those of us still squealing away in the nursery. Sure, we resemble him in some ways, but we are most definitely not him.

Make no mistake: the idea to call him our Father was not some intricately planned con of the church to make the message of a confusing God a bit more palatable. No. It was God's idea. He called himself our Father and called us his children. Now why would he do that? Does he not often restrain himself from preventing incredible suffering in the world? What kind of Father would do such a thing? It is the kind of Father whose viewpoint encompasses a spiritual reality and perspective often foreign to us. A nursery window if you will. He thinks thoughts billions of stratospheres higher than those of us still just trying to open our eyes in the new world.

You may have just shuddered at my statement. We do not like being compared to children. Immature. Ignorant. Missing the point and missing the school bus. I mean no disrespect; I only mean that we must understand that if the state we live in while walking the course of humanity is truly a spiritual childhood—a glance at truth through a window dark and dim—then our own experiences with our own children easily show us that there is a discrepancy between what the parent understands and what the child understands.

There is a key limit to this comparison. Unlike our own children, we will never fully *grow up* to be exactly like our heavenly Father. Why? Because our earthly examples are all still . . . well, earthly. Every parent on this earth has or has had a parent on this earth who also had a parent. Every adult was once a child. Every scholar once sucked his or her own thumb.

God? He has no parent. He has no beginning. He has no infancy. Humanity can never attain to this level because we are made only in his *likeness*, not in his *exactness*, or else we never needed to be created in the first place.

THE DIFFERENCES BETWEEN
FATHERS AND DADDIES

God's creation of humanity and his own title of Father began in Genesis and continued throughout the Old Testament. In Deuteronomy 32:6 (NLT), Moses asks the question, "Isn't he your Father who created you? Has he not made you and established you?" Early on the followers of God understood that he was not just their God; he was their Father. David even called him a "Father to the fatherless, defender of widows—this is God, whose dwelling is holy. God places the lonely in families; he sets the prisoners free and gives them joy" (Ps. 68:5–6 NLT). Can you see the ultimate Father figure, fathering those who have no one to turn to and even helping the lonely find refuge in a family? Again, the concept of a father-God is not solely a modern one.

Time would not permit me to list all the times Jesus referred to God as his Father. The New Testament is riddled with these references, even calling God our *Abba* (Rom. 8:15), a Hebrew term for "Father" that would be the English equivalent of a young child calling her father "Daddy."

Daddy, eh? Now, that changes things a bit for the road-weary life traveler who cannot seem to stomach the concept of a father-God who is distant, ominous, and foreboding. He has no idea that God is a Daddy who is eager to embrace his little one—the spittin' image of him.

> GOD IS A DADDY WHO IS EAGER TO EMBRACE HIS LITTLE ONE—THE SPITTIN' IMAGE OF HIM.

I have a biological father, but he definitely was not my daddy. My daddy was the man who chose me, who brought me into his home, even if he didn't bring me into the world. My face may resemble my father's, but my life resembles my daddy's. I talk as he does. I think as he does. I act as he does.

Most of the world knows God as a biological father but not as a daddy. Abandoned children often resent the characteristics they share with their biological parents as if those characteristics are nothing more than cruel reminders that they were not loved enough to be kept. Thus, a world resents the standards and morals it inherited from creation's Father, mostly because they have no idea that God is more than a father; he's a daddy.

This is the focal point of my entire life. I've written this book just so I could tell you this: my God has done more than just produce you; he has

> **GOD IS BOTH FATHER AND DADDY, BOTH POWERFUL CREATOR AND GENTLE CARETAKER.**

also chosen you. Dominic was mine. My child. My choice. My chance. I became more than just a father to that little wrinkly boy in the hospital; I became his daddy. That's how it is with God. He is both Father and Daddy, both powerful Creator and gentle Caretaker.

BIG DADDY

When Michelle and I took Dominic home, I learned that being a daddy was not always easy. It required patience and understanding. I also learned that one should never yawn at 3:00 a.m. while changing a little boy's diaper. That little guy was a good shot, and I swear that he was laughing at me when he let the "yellow river" flow! I'm still holding it against him, mainly because I still feel like vomiting every time I think about it.

But that's Daddydom—full of good moments and bad moments. Way-to-go's, no-no's, and oh-no's. Having my own son solidified my belief that God had brought me full circle from the twenty-dollar bastard kid. I was now the father I never had. I am not a perfect dad, not by any stretch of the imagination. However, I can guarantee you that my boy knows how much his daddy loves him.

It was during this time of life that the opportunities to speak came more frequently, at much bigger venues than I had ever imagined. I continued to speak in public school assemblies, but I also began to be booked to share my story at large youth camps and conventions. One day I would speak to a small school of four hundred students, and the next night I would speak at a convention of four thousand. Then even larger organizations began calling, and I found myself sharing stages on football fields with guys like Billy Graham and at Promise Keeper events. I began to speak to crowds of thirty to forty thousand people on a regular basis.

There was a point in my life when it would have been easy to revel in the glory of it all. What a story! A young black man pulls himself up from nothing to speak to hundreds of thousands of people each week. In many ways, I was tempted to feel as though I had *arrived*. However, I never forgot the journey that brought me to that point and the passion I had been given. And that little boy back at home was the most effective reminder of who God had called me to be: a daddy.

That is why I never stopped journeying into the trenches of the public schools. My passion lives within their walls because that is where the students are. I may be a biological daddy to only one kid, but I am determined to offer myself as an adopted daddy of sorts to any kid out there who needs to understand the love of a father . . . and of *the* Father.

Sometimes I wonder why kids want to listen to an old dude who does not know them from Adam. Deep down inside, I know why: it is because I love them, and they know it. The love for them inside of me is bigger than I am; it was placed there by the cosmic Daddy.

So they request me as their MySpace and Facebook friends by the tens of thousands. They write me letters. They send me messages. They follow me on Twitter. Though I am incapable of communicating personally with each of them every day, I really try to commit myself to reply and respond to the individual because it is the individual that matters. That is just what a daddy does.

PRICELESS ONES

We live in a society where the value of one-dollar bills is not what it used to be. Much of this is due to inflation, but much of it is also because it is easy to only think of large bills as valuable. One-dollar bills are what we receive when we break the larger, more worthwhile bills. Prove it? Okay. If I advertised an event where I was going to give away a random cash prize for all those who showed up, and I whipped out a one-dollar bill, there would be "boos" galore. People just do not value the *ones* as much anymore.

However, it is the value of the one-dollar bill that gives the other larger bills their worth. A twenty-dollar bill is made up of twenty one-dollar bills. The single dollar is still the base. In fact, the dollar is the foundation of our entire economic system. Have you ever heard an economic report that stated that the value of *the* dollar was up or down? They do not say that the value of hundred-dollar bills is up or down. It is the *one* that still matters.

We have also forgotten the value of the *one* person. The *one* is the foundation of God's value system for humanity too. As a public speaker I find it is so easy to focus my energies on the masses or to convince myself that there is more value in larger numbers. But that is not how a daddy feels. A daddy knows that each child is valuable beyond description. My heart overflows with the realization that God, the eternal Father, is longing for each individual out there to realize his or her worth in his eyes, to know that each one matters to him, individually, one at a time.

The best way to let people know they matter to *God* is to let them know they matter to *me*. That is why I will go anywhere, from the huge inner-city schools of New York City to the frozen plains of Ellendale, North Dakota. The value of my journey—of my calling—is accumulated one priceless individual at a time. Sure, I speak to tens of thousands, but God has called me to see the value of the one.

I learned this best while speaking at a conference called Winterfest in Knoxville, Tennessee, many years ago. It was a great homecoming to head back to where I grew up and speak at the Thompson-Boling Arena, where I had watched the Volunteers and Lady Volunteers basketball teams play so many games. The arena was packed with more than twenty thousand students and adults—literally a sea of humanity.

But there was one student who caught my heart that night. I had just finished my message and had invited students to meet with counselors in various parts of the arena to discuss and pray about what they had heard. Thousands responded, but I felt strongly led by God to focus my attention on one young man who was seated in the upper bleachers. He was all the way up in section 321. I could barely make him out from where I was standing, but I knew he was *the one* God wanted me to go find.

> THE BEST WAY TO LET PEOPLE KNOW THEY MATTER TO GOD *IS TO LET* THEM KNOW THEY MATTER TO ME.

It was quite a journey all the way up there, even for a natural athlete like me. (Hey! I can hear you snickering!) Anyway, I had to ride up two escalators and climb about a hundred steps to make it to his row. I had a few event people walking with me, but I was on a singular mission. It was *my* mission.

He had a hoodie pulled over his head and was completely oblivious to my presence. I scooted my way through the crowded row and patted his shoulder. "Hey, man, are you okay?"

He freaked out! Almost jumping out of his skin, he let out a slew of F-bombs. Cuss words stopped shocking me a long time ago. I knew that the issues in his life were deeper and more complicated than a couple words of profanity.

"I just came up here to help you; that's all. I felt like God wanted me to come find you."

He changed in an instant. He broke down and began crying like a little baby, sniffling and wiping his nose on his sleeve. "Dude, I'm messed up. I don't know God anymore, and my life is out of control. I saw you speaking tonight to these thousands of people. I was watching you on the JumboTron, and I told God, 'If you still love me, send that guy up here and have him ask me if I'm okay.'"

More tears. I was floored; but it got deeper. The young man reached into his sweatshirt and pulled out a handgun. My heart was beating out of my chest, but I tried to remain calm. He continued. "I brought this here tonight because I thought my life was over, and I was going to kill myself right here at Winterfest in front of everyone, but God loves me! He really *loves* me!"

I reached out and took the gun from his trembling hand and gave it to one of the event workers who had accompanied me. The worker's face was priceless but not as much as that one young man who had sat broken and lost in a sea of faces and now grasped just how valuable he truly was. He was not lost to his heavenly Daddy. God knew right where he was and was listening to the cries of the boy's desperate heart. The whole world had missed him up to that point, but God had *not* forgotten him.

My role is to listen and hear the voice of the one crying out among a million others because to God that one is . . . well, one in a million.

THE VALUE OF SCARS

At the time of this writing, Dominic is about to graduate from high school and set out into the world on his own journey. He already has been with me all over the world on various speaking engagements. He is the pride of my life. He is my buddy.

I will never forget what the doctor said that day when our boy was giving us fits inside his mommy and seemingly had no intention of coming out quietly. "I'm going to have to give your wife a scar if they are going to survive." Michelle and I both agree that Dominic was worth the scars!

How much more are you and I worth the scars Jesus bears? He was ripped up like an old T-shirt so that we could survive. The day Jesus laid down his life for us was the day God showed the world that he was more than just a biological father who begat us. He was not just a distant Creator who was disinterested and disappointed in us. On that day, he *chose* us.

Now you have heard my story, but what about yours? I have had to fight to be a hero and to overcome the stigma of my past; you must fight too. If I can make it, if God can find the value of this little nobody among the billions in the world, then you can rest assured that he knows you too. You may not be a religious person; in fact, I kind of hope you are not because often what we bring to the table from our religious past is stale and no longer good for eating. The table you are being invited to is a family table, decorated and set with sustenance for your soul. It is a feast of grace and significance, tasted only in your dreams.

The price of admission to this feast? Well, for you it's free. You can sit down, stuff a napkin inside the collar of your shirt, and pig out on the future God has laid out for you. You can delight yourself in the abundance of his forgiveness. You can know the hero that he is and the hero that he is making of you. You can discover that your past is unchangeable, but your future is still up for grabs. You can know your value and your passion. You can know your Father.

Yeah, the meal is free but only for you. It is actually the most expensive spread ever purchased. So what is the cost of your freedom, the opportunity to be healed of your past and to embrace a future you don't deserve? It cost Jesus his very life. If you have heard that before and immediately want to roll your eyes because you have read it on every church marquee in your town, or you have possibly had it shoved down your throat by those who are well meaning but still ineffective, then you are the one in danger of bringing stale bread to this table.

It might be an all-too familiar idea to you, or it might be a brand-new concept. Either way, knowing the truth about Jesus and what he did for you is the key to living the kind of life I have been telling you about throughout this book. Forget for a moment that you have ever heard the story, and let Reggie lay it out for you one more time.

Jesus was God's Son. He lived in a perfect place with perfect power. Against all odds, he chose to leave that perfection and place himself within the imperfection of humanity. In a body just like yours. He sneezed. He got tired. He got angry. He faced disappointment. Yet in all of this he did something we could never do: he avoided anything that would separate him from God.

That might not seem huge to you, but it really was. Why? He made himself our *perfect* representative before God. He could speak and act on our behalf because he was human, yet he could speak and act on God's behalf because he was God—and he was perfect in both respects. The go-between. The ultimate peacemaker. The divine mediator. Our agent of mercy.

Then he did the unexpected. He decided that he would let the sentence placed on our lives because of our sin be executed by him, literally. We deserved to die, but he died for us instead. Not just any death, but the most excruciating death imaginable. How bad was it? Put it this way: the word *ex*-cruci-*ating* is literally derived from the Latin word *cruci* or "cross." Simply put, when a word was needed that would be the very definition of the most intense pain one can experience, *cross* was the word they came up with.

Was the cross fair? No. Was it love? Oh, yes! Was it by his choice? Yes. In other words, you were his choice, and you were worth enough to him that he was willing to die in your place.

The best part, though, was that he did not stay dead! He came back to life to complete and continue that which he started with those who will choose to accept the free gift of life that he has purchased for them. Man, that's some high price he paid! You must be worth much more than you know.

In the end it is about your value to the Father. It is about realizing that the wrists and back of his Son are brutally scarred so that you can be assured that he loves you and knows your name. You are his needle in the haystack of this world. You are his one in a million. You are his Gomer. You are his Reggie. You are his heart because you are his child, fashioned in his image. You are his.

Take it from a guy who has no business being alive, much less living a life of meaning and significance: you can't change your past, but he can change your future. His scars prove it.

Questions for Individual and Group Reflection

1. How do you think Reggie and Michelle felt when they experienced difficulty in the delivery process of their son?

   _____

   _____

2. What emotions do parents generally feel concerning their children? How do these feelings shape the lives of parents and children alike?

   _____

   _____

3. Do you think the concept of God being a father is biblically accurate? Have we exaggerated it in today's culture?

   _____

   _____

4. What are your reactions to the fatherhood statistics?

   _____

   _____

5. How has our concept of "father" affected your view of God?

   _____

   _____

6. Have you ever thought about the fact that the individual dollar is the foundation of our economy? What are the spiritual parallels to this concept?

_____

_____

7. Do you agree with Reggie's point that we are made in God's image? What parts of humanity (even when humanity does not acknowledge God) are made in God's image?

_____

_____

8. Do you really think God is that concerned over the value of one individual? Why or why not?

_____

_____

9. Concerning the guy at the Winterfest event, how might his story have been different without someone seeing that young man's individual value?

_____

_____

10. What has Reggie's story shown you about your own story? Examine your relationship with God. Do you need to realign yourself at the family table of the Father?

_____

_____

Chapter 10: Big Daddy

1. National Fatherhood Initiative, "Fatherhood Statistics," http://www.fatherhood.org/Page.aspx?pid=330.
2. U.S. Census Bureau, "Children's Living Arrangements and Characteristics: March 2002," P200-547, Table C8 (Washington, DC: GPO, 2003).
3. Elaine and Chava Zibman, "Getting to Know Poor Fathers Who Do Not Pay Child Support," *Social Service Review*, vol. 75 (September 2001), 420–34.
4. James A. Gaudino Jr., Bill Jenkins, and Foger W. Rochat, "No Fathers' Names: A Risk Factor for Infant Mortality in the State of Georgia, USA," *Social Science and Medicine*, vol. 48 (1999), 253–65.
5. John Cairney, Michael Boyle, et al., "Stress, Social Support and Depression in Single and Married Mothers," *Social Psychiatry and Psychiatric Epidemiology*, vol. 38 (August 2003), 442–49.
6. T. O'Connor, L. Davies, J. Dunn, J. Golding, ALSPAC Study Team, "Differential Distribution of Children's Accidents, Injuries and Illnesses Across Family Type," *Pediatrics*, vol. 106 (November 2000), 68.
7. Steven P. Cuffe, Robert E. McKeown, Cheryl L. Addy, and Carol Z. Garrison, "Family Psychosocial Risk Factors in a Longitudinal Epidemiological Study of Adolescents," *Journal of American Academic Child Adolescent Psychiatry*, vol. 44 (February 2005), 121–29.
8. Kristin Harknett, "Children's Elevated Risk of Asthma in Unmarried Families: Underlying Structural and Behavioral Mechanisms," Working Paper #2005-01-FF (Princeton, NJ: Center for Research on Child Well-being, 2005), 19–27.
9. Cynthia C. Harper and Sara S. McLanahan, "Father Absence and Youth Incarceration," *Journal of Research on Adolescence*, vol. 14 (September 2004), 369–97.

10. Doris J. James, "Profile of Jail Inmates, 2002 (NCJ 201932)," Bureau of Justice Statistics Special Report, Department of Justice, Office of Justice Programs, July 2004.
11. Tracy L. Snell and Danielle C. Morton, "Women in Prison: Survey of Prison Inmates, 1991," Bureau of Justice Statistics Special Report (Washington, DC: U.S. Department of Justice, 1994), 4.
12. John P. Hoffmann, "The Community Context of Family Structure and Adolescent Drug Use," *Journal of Marriage and Family*, vol. 64 (May 2002), 314–30.
13. Jacinta Bronte-Tinkew, Kristin A. Moore, Randolph C. Capps, and Jonathan Zaff, "The influence of father involvement on youth risk behaviors among adolescents: A comparison of native-born and immigrant families," *Press, Social Science Research* (December 2004).
14. Kenneth W. Griffin, Gilbert J. Botvin, Lawrence M. Scheier, Tracy Diaz, and Nicole L. Miller, "Parenting Practices as Predictors of Substance Use, Delinquency, and Aggression Among Urban Minority Youth: Moderating Effects of Family Structure and Gender," *Psychology of Addictive Behaviors*, vol. 14 (June 2000), 174–84.
15. Jay D. Teachman, "The Childhood Living Arrangements of Children and the Characteristics of Their Marriages," *Journal of Family Issues*, vol. 25 (January 2004), 86–111.
16. Robert J. Quinlan, "Father absence, parental care, and female reproductive development," *Evolution and Human Behavior*, vol. 24 (November 2003), 376–90.
17. Ibid.
18. Bruce J. Ellis, John E. Bates, Kenneth A. Dodge, David M. Ferguson, L. John Horwood, Gregory S. Pettit, and Lianne Woodward, "Does Father Absence Place Daughters at Special Risk for Early Sexual Activity and Teenage Pregnancy?" *Child Development*, vol. 74 (May/June 2003), 801–21.
19. "America's Children: Key National Indicators of Well-Being," Table SPECIAL1 (Washington, DC: Federal Interagency Forum on Child and Family Statistics, 1997).
20. Andrea J. Sedlak and Diane D. Broadhurst, "The Third

National Incidence Study of Child Abuse and Neglect: Final Report," (Washington, DC: U.S. Department of Health and Human Services, National Center on Child Abuse and Neglect, September 1996).

21. U.S. Department of Health and Human Services, National Center for Health Statistics, Survey on Child Health (Washington, DC: GPO, 1993).

22. Christine Winquist Nord and Jerry West, "Fathers' and Mothers' Involvement in Their Children's Schools by Family Type and Resident Status (NCES 2001–032)" (Washington, DC: U.S. Department of Education, National Center for Education Statistics, 2001).

23. Laura Lippman et al., "Indicators of Child, Family, and Community Connections, Office of the Assistant Secretary for Planning and Evaluation" (Washington, DC: U.S. Department of Health and Human Services, 2004).

24. National Center for Education Statistics, "The Condition of Education (NCES 1999022)" (Washington, DC: U.S. Department of Education, 1999), 76.

25. Brent A. McBride, Sarah K. Schoppe-Sullivan, and Moon-Ho Ho, "The mediating role of fathers' school involvement on student achievement," *Applied Developmental Psychology*, vol. 26 (2005), 201–16.

ABOUT THE AUTHORS

Reggie Dabbs has been one of the most sought-after public school and event speakers in the United States and the world for more than two decades. Reggie relentlessly chases his personal passion around the globe by sharing his own astonishing story of tragedy, redemption, and hope with millions of people each year, from professional athletes and stay-at-home moms to high school students. An acclaimed saxophonist, Reggie lives in Ft. Myers, Florida, with Michelle, his wife of twenty years, and their son, Dominic.

Follow Reggie on Twitter and Facebook.

For event booking information,
check out www.reggiedabbsonline.com
or www.cinderent.com.

For school bookings,
contact www.theyouthalliance.com
or 1-888-480-7592.

John Driver is a husband, father, pastor, author, and songwriter. He and his wife, Laura, along with their daughter, Sadie, live in Mt. Juliet, Tennessee, near Nashville.

Follow John on Twitter and Facebook.

To subscribe to John's blog
or to book him to speak at an event,
check out www.johndriver.net.